BestMasters

Springer awards „BestMasters" to the best master's theses which have been completed at renowned Universities in Germany, Austria, and Switzerland.
The studies received highest marks and were recommended for publication by supervisors. They address current issues from various fields of research in natural sciences, psychology, technology, and economics.
The series addresses practitioners as well as scientists and, in particular, offers guidance for early stage researchers.

Ann-Kathrin Lehnhausen

Studies on Competition and Antitrust Issues in the Pharmaceutical Industry

With a preface by Dr. Johannes Paha

Springer Gabler

Ann-Kathrin Lehnhausen
Gießen, Germany

BestMasters
ISBN 978-3-658-16550-5 ISBN 978-3-658-16551-2 (eBook)
DOI 10.1007/978-3-658-16551-2

Library of Congress Control Number: 2016959244

Springer Gabler

Printed on acid-free paper

This Springer Gabler imprint is published by Springer Nature
The registered company is Springer Fachmedien Wiesbaden GmbH
The registered company address is: Abraham-Lincoln-Str. 46, 65189 Wiesbaden, Germany

Preface

The pharmaceutical industry has increasingly moved into the focus of antitrust authorities. Allegations of anticompetitive conduct by drug manufacturers can be read in the news every week. This is because innovative drugs are frequently offered by just one firm holding a dominant position in the respective sub-market.

Initially, such a position may be granted by patent rights and other forms of protection of intellectual property (IP). The market power (i.e., prices above variable production costs) being established by IP laws helps pharmaceutical companies to earn revenues covering the research and development expenses incurred not only for the marketed drugs but also for drugs that never made it to the market. Insofar, some degree of market power for a predefined period of time appears necessary such that the pharmaceutical companies invest in research in the first place.

But what is an appropriate price for the drug? What happens if a drug company differentiates prices by setting the regular price in countries with a high per-capita gross domestic product (GDP) and grants a discount in countries with a low per-capita GDP? In such a situation, wholesalers might be tempted to re-import the drug from the low-income country and sell it in the high-income country. The pharmaceutical company might react by removing discounts in the low income country, unless it can restrain trade between these two countries. This raises the question whether trade restrictions and price discrimination are detrimental to welfare.

A further question concerns firms' strategies after the expiry of a patent. What strategies do incumbent firms use to prevent entrants from seeking access to the market? For example, one might think of payments made by the incumbents and received by the entrants for delaying market entry. How do such agreements affect welfare? Answering these questions is not trivial even in industries other than the pharmaceutical industry. Answers are even harder to find for the drug market that is not only subject to control by antitrust authorities. It is also protected by IP laws, regulated by government authorities, and characterized by powerful buyers such as health insurance companies.

Ms. Lehnhausen took the challenge to discuss the effects of anticompetitive conduct in this industry. Such an analysis requires presenting its specificities, including, e.g., a description of the research and development process, the buyer-seller-relationships in this market, and its regulatory environment. This excellent description will be informative for readers looking for an overview about this market.

Based on this presentation, Ms. Lehnhausen presents anticompetitive conduct taken by one firm alone (e.g., vertical restraints such as resale price maintenance, or strategies aimed at restraining the entry of producers of generics). Then, she discusses interactions between two or more firms (e.g., pay-for-delay agreements or mergers). Most importantly, she goes beyond merely listing these types of conduct but reviews state-of-the-art research on the welfare effects of these competitive restraints. These chapters, which account for about two thirds of the book, may be interesting also for readers who already know this market well and want to learn more about its recent discussion in the economics literature.

This book is a revised version of Ms. Lehnhausen's Master thesis submitted to Justus-Liebig-University Giessen. Being an assistant professor at the Chair for Industrial Organization, Regulation, and Antirust, I had the pleasure to supervise her thesis. I enjoyed seeing the progress that she made when writing it, and I found it quite informative. It was a pleasure learning that the editors at *Springer Verlag* thought the same way when they offered to publish the thesis in their BestMasters series. I am confident that this book will not disappoint its readers.

Dr. Johannes Paha

Giessen, August 25, 2016

Prologue

This publication is a revised version of the Master's Thesis I wrote for my Master's degree in Business Administration at Justus-Liebig-University Giessen. The ideas for this project arose after an internship I did at a pharmaceutical company, in which I learned more about pricing of pharmaceuticals. Through this internship, I realized that prices for pharmaceuticals are not only defined by the manufacturer and the regulating authority but are also influenced by wholesalers and pharmacists to some extent.

Together with my advisor, Dr. Johannes Paha, I decided to study this pricing of pharmaceutical products, with focus on branded drugs in more detail. During the research, I did not only find out how costs for research and development of originator drugs arise but also came across anticompetitive actions of originator drug producers that lead to extended exclusivity time on the market and hence to extended time of monopoly pricing. Pay for delay settlements and product hopping were the first actions I examined, and with a more detailed research, I was able to find additional competition deterring actions. However, I also found out that drug companies often tried to justify these actions, which foremost seemed to harm welfare without exception, by stating that innovation cost for drugs were increasing and extended exclusivity time was needed to cover those costs.

Based on this literature research, my central question was, why prices for originator drugs are increasing every year and which actions to deter competition of cheaper drugs substitutes exist. Moreover, as pharmaceutical manufacturers often mention high development cost for innovative drugs, my intention was to find out, if there are also positive welfare effects arising from these anticompetitive actions.

Consequently, this publication gives a precise overview about market structure of the pharmaceutical industry, the costs for development of innovative drugs, and anticompetitive actions performed by originator manufacturers. In addition to that, it also gives an indication, which of these actions can even be beneficial for consumers and which actions should be analyzed more strictly by authorities in order to prevent excessive increase on public healthcare spending.

In this context, I would like to thank my advisor Dr. Johannes Paha for his support and for challenging me to grow beyond myself, enabling me to write this book.

I would also like to thank Michael, Silvia and Volker for their support; For giving me incentives to go on in times of doubt, for their endless patience, their unconditional love and for always believing in me.

Ann-Kathrin Lehnhausen

Braunfels, August 27, 2016

Table of Content

Table of Figures

Table of Abbreviations

ACEA	European Automobile Manufacturers Association
ADR	Adverse Drug Reactions
CDER	Center for Dug Evaluation Research
EFPIA	European Federation of Pharmaceutical Industries and Associations
EMA	European Medical Agency
EUR	Euro
FDA	Food and Drug Administration
FTC	Federal Trade Commission
GRP	Generic Reference Pricing
GSK	GlaxoSmithKline LLC
IFPMA	International Federation of Pharmaceutical Manufacturers and Associations
IMS Health	Institute for Healthcare Informatics
IPR	Intellectual Property Rights
M&A	Merger and Acquisition
OTC	Over-The-Counter
PBM	Pharmaceutical Business Manager
Phrma	Pharmaceutical Research and Manufacturers of America
PCR	Price Cap Regulation
PD	Parkinson's Disease
R&D	Research and Development
RLS	Restless Legs Syndrome

RPR	Reference Price Regulation
RPM	Resale Price Maintenance
SGB	Sozialgesetzbuch
SPC	Supplementary Protection Certificate
TFEU	Treaty on the Functioning of the European Union
TRP	Therapeutic Reference Pricing
U.S.C.	United States Code
USD	United States Dollar
VI	Vertical Integration
€	Euro
$	United States Dollar

1. Introduction

The increase of healthcare expenditures faced by the public sector is one of the most discussed topics in the last century. According to researchers, this increase in spending is mainly due to the fact, that prices for pharmaceuticals and therefore expenditures for pharmaceutical products have risen over the past decade (Bardeya, Bommier and Jullien 2010: 303). Not only was this a result of an intensification in research and development (R&D) in the 1980s and 1990s through cooperation between private and public sectors (Cockburn & Henderson 2001: 30). It was also due to the fact that pharmaceutical firms tried to produce more innovative products which assured patent protection and market power, leading to increased drug prices in order to gain high revenues. Furthermore, as signaling effect for product quality, manufacturers increased price even after patent protection (Garattini, Motterlini and Cornago 2008: 305). One of many examples for such a drug price increase is Turing Pharmaceuticals, raising the price for their parasite defending drug Daraprim by over 5,000 percent (Jaffe 2015: 2127; Perlman 2015).

Contemporaneously to the increased investments in innovation, a significant increase in production and prescription of less expensive substitutes, so-called generic drugs, could be observed (Comanor and Scherer 2013: 106). This growth in both, R&D and generic production is not contradictory but a consequence of one another. Increase in innovation and patent protection leads to monopoly power and high profits of manufacturers (Bennato and Valletti 2014: 84). Hence, possible entrants are attracted. With the termination of patent protection competition arises and substitute products can enter the market. Consequently, innovators' interest is to further invest in R&D to get patent protection and monopoly power which will attract additional substitute producers to enter the market (Garattini, Motterlini and Cornago 2008: 305; Comanor and Scherer 2013: 106). However, not only does generic market entry impose competition to the innovating manufacturers. Parallel traded drugs do also impose competition in prices, even before the patent terminated (Graslandt and Maskus 2004: 1036).

My objective, therefore, is to analyze all actions performed by innovating drug manufactures to deter competition and sidestep regulations, in the context of antitrust and competition law in the US and EU. By showing anticompetitive actions undertaken by innovating firms, this paper will also give an indication for regulatory institutions, how to improve statutory provisions, to hinder anticompetitive actions and thus reduce healthcare expenditures due to reduced prices for pharmaceuticals because of increased competition.

Competition leads to an increase in pressure on the innovating companies as their incentive is to generate high profits to cover their R&D costs while simultaneously being able to compete with cheaper substitutes. In addition to this pressure to generate maximum profits, pharmaceutical companies also face the problem, that they have to meet requirements predefined by regulating authorities in order to be allowed to sell their drugs (Kaiser et al. 2014: 174). Those regulations can vary significantly across countries and influences the price setting of drug manufacturers. Innovators have to adjust their pricing strategies to the regulatory provisions in each country. Regulators' intention is to reduce the prices for pharmaceuticals because the cheaper a treatment for diseases gets, the less a consumer needs to spend on healthcare. Particularly competition after patent expiration reduces innovators' revenues, which they need to cover R&D costs. Since the reduction of pharmaceutical prices is dependent on the intensity of competition and regulatory provisions regulators are prone to support this competition. Thus, research intensive manufacturers have an incentive to prevent other market participants from entering the market or rather to not even serve certain markets, where price regulations are restrictive. An action that can be often observed in this context, is that innovating drug manufacturers achieve extended market exclusivity through extended patent protection. Consequently, it needs to be analyzed how innovating companies can thwart market entry of competitors and circumvent statutory provisions. The pharmaceutical market, is one of the most complex markets to analyze because of its multilayered interactions of participants that need to be considered. Influence on price increases and changes in healthcare spending, hence, cannot only be reduced to one monopoly firm trying to increase its profit as extensively as possible. It is rather to be traced back to the interaction of more than one firm in different market situations. Whereas the manufacturer can be in a monopoly and a perfect competitive situation at the same time. This occurs when the company offers products that are patent protected and products that ran out of patent protection (Puig-Junoy 2010: 650). Furthermore, the market does not just consist of one supply and one demand side, where the supplier gets paid by the individual who demands the good. There rather exist additional market participants that pay for the goods demanded by the patient and retail the drugs supplied by the pharmaceutical firm (Pedroso and Nakano 2009: 378). This intensifies the pressure on pharmaceutical firms to meet the demands of every market participant while simultaneously gaining enough revenue to cover innovation cost, on the one hand. (DiMasi 2002: 2). On the other hand, it creates opportunities for R&D intensive manufacturers to circumvent regulatory provisions.

To understand why pharmaceutical producers, violate free market competition requires comprehension of this complexity of pharmaceutical markets. Therefore, I will first give an overview of the pharmaceutical market structure including all parties that influence the supply and demand side of drugs. This overview will present common facts about the size of the pharmaceutical market, the Research and Development (R&D) process, how costs for pharmaceutical products emerge and the different parties that interact and define prices for the drugs. Subsequently, my objective is to present a model of the pharmaceutical market including the possibilities of innovating drug manufacturers to restrain competition and extend exclusive market rights.

The third chapter, then, presents different actions of pharmaceutical firms that hinder competition in order to gain higher market shares and deter entry. This part of the paper will primarily focus on actions taken by one single firm. In detail, I will examine anticompetitive actions where the innovating company restricts free trade and competition. The chapter is divided into three parts that focus on different initial situations of the manufacturer. The first part discusses actions that restrict parallel trade. The second part analyzes competition restrictions und regulatory provisions in different states and the last part focuses on anticompetitive actions involving extension of patent protection.

Chapter 4, in contrast, examines antitrust violating actions that result from interaction between the innovating firm and one or more firms that produce perfect substitutes to the R&D intensive firm's products. In this part, I will differentiate between the so-called pay for delay settlements and Merger and Acquisition (M&A). Both chapters specially discuss the circumvention of antitrust law in the context of extension of market exclusivity and show that they result from some of the, in chapter three discussed mechanisms. I will give a recommendation on how antitrust authorities can prevent infringements of competitions law and when staving off competition can be profitable for consumers by not jeopardizing pharmaceutical companies' incentives to invest in R&D.

2. The Pharmaceutical Industry

Understanding the actions taken by pharmaceutical firms in order to thwart competition requires the information on how the pharmaceutical sector is constructed. The pharmaceutical market, referred to in this paper, contains all firms that produce or develop pharmaceuticals or compounds that are used to produce drugs and all other participants that interact with those firms for the purpose of selling or purchasing a drug, not regarding other healthcare products. Furthermore, understanding of which market participants exist and how important it is for an economy to keep this sector growing by supporting its production and development, is required to understand anticompetitive actions performed by pharmaceutical innovators. This chapter will give an overview on the above defined market, how drugs are developed and launched, how costs for drugs are assembled and on the constituents of pharmaceutical firms' costs. As a conclusion, section 2.5 will show why firms have a motivation to prevent competition and which actions innovating drug manufacturers can choose to thwart competition.

2.1 Facts and Figures

The modern pharmaceutical industry is fairly profitable. In 2014, total revenues of the world pharmaceutical market added up to about € 965.03 billion[1] and is expected to reach € 1,159.7 billion[2] in 2018 (IMS Health 2015: 1; IMS Health 2014: 5). Exports of pharmaceutical goods are important for the economy of developed countries. In 2014, for example, pharmaceutical exports in Europe amounted to € 316,000 million. According to the European Federation of Pharmaceutical Industries and Associations (EFPIA), pharmaceutical imports, however, were only € 238.5 billion, leaving a Trade balance of € 78 billion (2015: 2). In comparison, the European automotive sector showed a trade balance of € 95.1 billion, with € 124.2 billion exports and € 29.1 billion imports (European Automobile Manufacturers Association (ACEA) 2015: 50). Although the automotive industry exhibited a higher trade balance, the overall amount of money circulating was much higher in the pharmaceutical sector. This proves the importance of the pharmaceutical sector for the European economy.

---

[1] This value is converted from United States-Dollar ($) (USD) to Euro (€) (EUR), referring to the exchange rate of 1st August, 2015, because that date's exchange rate approximates the average value exchange rate of 2015. The referencing value published by Institute for Healthcare Informatics (IMS Health) (2015) amounts to $1,057.1 billion.

[2] This value is converted from USD to EUR, referencing to the exchange rate of January 8th, 2016. The referencing value published by IMS Health (2014) amounts to $ 1,300 billion.

The pharmaceutical industry, in addition to that, does not only contribute to high export rates within the European Union but the market is one of the most important employers worldwide (Ostwald, Zubrzycki, and Knippel 2015: 5). For example, according to Ostwald, Zubrzycki, and Knippel (2015: 15) in 2012, about 4.4 million people were employed in the pharmaceutical sector globally (which corresponds to about the whole population of New Zealand in 2012 (The Worldbank 2016)).

Additional to its importance in economic trade, the pharmaceutical sector is one of the most important sectors in Research and Development (R&D) matters. This is consistent with the findings of Dubois et al. who conclude that the intensity of innovation grows with market size (2015: 848). The European Commission states that in 2015, more than five pharmaceutical companies were amongst the top 20 of the firms with the world's highest spending on innovation (2015: 43). With Novartis as number five, spending € 8.3 million on R&D, and Roche (€ 7.4 billion), as well as Johnson&Johnson (€ 6.99 billion) following as number seven and eight, making the pharmaceutical industry one of the leading R&D sectors. In comparison to that, Volkswagen came in first, spending € 13.1 billion on R&D (European Commission 2015: 43). Even though no pharmaceutical company could reach number one of the most research intensive companies, the European Commission affirms that the pharmaceutical sector in total was the world's most research intensive sector in 2015 with more than € 100 billion spent on R&D. The automobile sector could only reach the second position with a spending of around € 90 billion (European Commission 2015: 50).

The R&D of new drugs is one of the main reasons why the pharmaceutical market is so important for many economies. The development of new drugs constitutes to the improvement of quality of life and the increase of life expectancy which both directly influence the welfare of an economy. At the same time R&D intensive manufacturers bare the risk of significant profit losses due to differences of profits before and after patent termination. Although there is high market potential in the pharmaceutical industry, many firms try to restrict other companies from competing for their market share by not only trying to develop differences to the goods offered by competitors but also paying the competitor to delay market entry (Kesselheim, Murtagh and Mello 2011: 1439). In order to comprehend why it is important for drug producing firms to reduce competition it is necessary to understand how the innovation process of pharmaceuticals works and how costs for development emerge, as presented in the following.

2.2 R&D Process and Cost Development

Before a newly innovated drug enters the market, it has to pass through several phases to prove that it does not endanger patients' lives because of side effects. It also needs to be proved, that the drug offers additional benefits in comparison to other pharmaceuticals that are already available on the market (Grabowski and Wann 2008: 379). The phases before the market launch of a drug can be divided into five basic phases, as is shown in Figure 1.

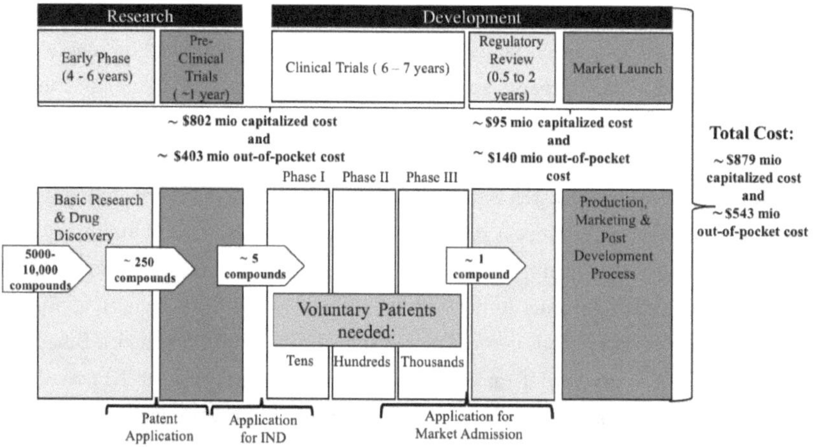

Figure 1: The Pharmaceutical R&D Process, own representation based on Center for Drug Evaluation and Research (CDER), 1998: 3; Phrma 2015: 45; DiMasi, Hansen, and Grabowski 2003: 173.

The first phase is the so-called "early phase". In this phase the R&D lab searches for promising compounds. The recent method for this search is to examine diseases for their pathogens which trigger the diseases in the human body. The goal is to find targets that weaken the pathogens and create compounds to develop a new drug or an improvement to an existing drug (Swinney and Anthony 2011: 507). A plethora of promising compounds are collected through open-innovation processes, collaborations with public laboratories and private research work (Cockburn and Henderson 2001: 12-15). According to the International Federation of Pharmaceutical Manufacturers and Associations (IFPMA)[3], it contains about 5000-10000 compounds (2014: 8). These compounds are screened for effectiveness and likelihood to become a successful medicine. At the end of the phase, after four to six years, about 250 compounds are taken under Intellectual Property Rights (IPR) protection for further development and finding of new pharmaceuticals. This means, producers get patent protection for their compounds (IFPMA 2014: 8).

3 Note: IPFMA is a pharmaceutical lobby organization. However, I refer to their publication as it gives a specific overview about development times of drugs which I was not able to find elsewhere.

After the early phase, there is a phase of pre-clinical testing. Within this phase, the compounds are tested for their efficacy to fight diseases. This examination is not yet performed on patients but rather on animals or in test tubes. The duration of this phase takes approximately one year and screens all compounds for clinical usage. At the end of the preclinical trials, there are typically around five compounds left, to apply for clinical trials. Those two early phases of pharmaceutical invention can be seen as the research part of the R&D process and together with the clinical trials amount to the greatest part of costs in the innovation process (Cockburn and Henderson 2001: 8; IFPMA 2014: 8; DiMasi, Hansen and Grabowski 2003: 173).

Following the phases of research is the phase of clinical trials. Clinical trials test the preparations for their effectiveness on the human body and examine if any other side effects concerning human health occur when using the compound (DiMasi, Hansen, and Grabowski 2003: 156). In order to perform the clinical trials, firms have to apply for Investigational New Drug (IND), to get permission for their test on patients. Since the clinical trials have to give proof for the safety and additional benefit of the new drug, independent physicians and researchers have to supervise the efficacy-tests on voluntary patients (Pharmaceutical Research and Manufacturers of America (Phrma) 2015: 46). The clinical trials can be divided into three sub-phases that are referred to as Phase I, Phase II and Phase III. The phases define the number of subjects tested on. If a compound is approved for the next phase, additional test subjects are required. Therefore, the number of voluntary patients required reaches up to thousands until phase three can be completed and the compound can apply for market approval (Grabowski and Wann 2008: 379). Overall, the clinical trials last for six to seven years on average. During the process, most of the compounds are eliminated because of safety issues for the human body and in the worst case scenarios there are no compounds left to apply for market admission. However, on average, there is one compound left that can apply for accreditation (IFPMA 2014: 8).

Before the drug can be launched on the market, a regulatory review board has to examine the drug's efficacy and cost-effectiveness. If the regulators give permission for market launch, which can take up to additional two years, the pharmaceutical can enter the market. Finally, after 12 to 14 years of R&D, the drug is available for patients and the main R&D investments are done (Cockburn and Henderson 2001: 8; IFPMA 2014: 8).

Patent protections usually lasts 20 years (35 United States Code (U.S.C) § 154 (a) (2); Article 63 European Patent Convention). In addition, data exclusivity for marketing of the pharmaceutical is granted, meaning no other company can use data on clinical trials and compounds to start developing a similar product. This exclusivity amounts to 11 years in the EU, according to the 8+2+1 rule. The rule grants an eight-year data exclusivity period, additional two years for exclusively marketing and a possibility to one year of extension. This ensures that the innovating company is granted 11 years of exclusivity, even if the patent already expires shortly after the drug launch (European Union[4]). In the US, however, manufacturers who gain market approval for innovative pharmaceuticals are granted 5 years of data and market exclusivity before any other company can access clinical trial data, according to U.S.C. Title 21 §355.

Applications for patents are submitted approximately 6 years after the screening of compounds (IFPMA 2014: 8). Then, there are seven to eight years needed for R&D, i.e. preclinical trials and the development phase of the R&D process. Hence, after the product is launched, a drug manufacturer has about 14 years of patent protection left, which is consistent with the findings of Grabowski and Kyle (2007: 497-499). Following Scott Morton and Margaret (2012: 772), the R&D expenses constitute the greatest part of the drug production process, imposing a large scale of fixed and sunk cost for the innovating company. Production cost of the drug generally only adds a small amount of marginal cost to the total cost of production. In this context, DiMasi and Grabowski (2007: 477) found, that the pre-clinical R&D process approximately amounts to $ 439 million capitalized cost on average and the clinical phases amount to about $ 879 million capitalized cost on average, leading to sunk cost for innovation of about $ 1318 million capitalized cost on average. Adams and Brantner (2006: 424), however, estimate total cost of innovation is about $ 802 million capitalized cost on average and DiMasi, Hansen, and Grabowskis' (2003: 173) analysis finds capitalized cost to amount to $ 897 million on average. This difference in estimates occurs due to the fact of different companies and drugs analyzed. Where DiMasi and Grabowski (2007: 477) analyze large US pharmaceutical producers, Adams and Brantner (2006: 424) examine pharmaceutical manufacturers with variations in size and value of drug. Nevertheless, both authors agree, that expenditures for R&D have risen over the past decades. This is consistent with the findings of DiMasi, Hansen, and Grabowski (2003: 162), stating that an increase in innovation costs can be observed due to the fact, that cost for clinical trials increased over the last decade, due to more treatments being available for patients. Therefore, more side-effects can occur because more than one or two drugs interact. Since the R&D process includes the largest part of production costs for pharmaceutical companies and profits can only be gained after the product is launched, firms have an incentive to keep the development time as short as possible in

---

4 See European Union (2004) 'Directive 2004/27/EC', *Official Journal of the European Union L 136/34*, URL: http://goo.gl/0eTbFJ (retrieved May 9, 2016).

order to gain as much patent protected time in the market as possible. After the patent protection has expired, other companies enter the market and competition starts, reducing profits for the innovating firm (Adriaen, De Witte and Simoens 2008: 176). Hence, the innovator has to generate as much profit as possible within the years of patent protection in order to compensate expenditures for R&D both, for the existing product and future products that may not ever make it to market and come at a loss to the firm. However, even if the basic process of pharmaceutical innovation is over, after the drug is launched, further costs arise for the life-cycle management of the good. Not only do firms need to advertise their product in order to raise their sales and refinance their investments spent on R&D (Brekke and Kuhn 2006: 103). But also due to pharmacovigilance, i.e. the monitoring of drug's side-effects and safeness, firms need to constantly adjust their products throughout the drug's lifetime. Pharmacovigilance has grown important for firms over the last few decades. It ensures that the intake and side-effects of drugs are monitored throughout the lifetime of a drug to ascertain safety and to detect Adverse Drug Reactions (ADR) that remain undetected during clinical trials (Grabowski and Wann 2008: 386). Even though there are three phases in pharmaceutical development that test the efficacy of the drug and its side-effects, some ADRs might not be discovered throughout the process of clinical testing (Sportiello et al. 2016: 731). In order to protect patients from suffering under unwanted and unknown side effects, firms have to strictly monitor possible harmful ADRs, which is supervised by the European Medicine Agency (EMA) in Europe and by the Food and Drug Administration (FDA) in the US (European Union 2010: 1[5] ; European Union 2010: 74[6]; FDA 2007[7]). As a result, in the EU patients, physicians and other healthcare professionals, pharmaceutical companies, and regulatory authorities are obliged to report any sign of ADR. Those indications of ADR can be reported to the pharmaceutical firm, which then has to report it directly to the authorities. Thus, every company has to position a pharmacovigilance officer that monitors any announcement of ADRs and passes this information on to the authorities (Sultana, Cutroneo and Trifirò 2013: 77). The pharmaceutical firm has to examine their drug to ascertain if the reported ADR is caused by the drug itself or by some other trigger. If the side effects are a result of the drugs' ingredients, the compound has to be changed (Sportiello, et al 2016: 731).

---

5 See European Union (2010), 'Regulation (EU) No. 1235/10 (1)', *Official Journal of the European Union L 348/1-16*, URL: http://goo.gl/XjnSlt (retrieved May 10, 2016).

6 See European Union (2010) 'Directive 2010/84 EU', *Official Journal of the European Union L 348/74-99*, URL: http://goo.gl/nVEB3k (retrieved May 10, 2016).

7 See Food and Drug Administration Amendments Act 2007 'Section 801 FDAAA', *121 STAT. 904 Public Law 110-85*, URL: https://goo.gl/L4Yvzm (retrieved May 10, 2016).

Finally, it can be said that the cost for drug development and adjustment after market launch are the main reasons for high expenditures on innovative medicine in the healthcare sector. Pharmaceutical companies, therefore, often try to justify high market prices with their high sunk cost for pre- and post- R&D expenditures. These prices constitute to high costs for insurance companies. One example for these high expenses for insurance companies are Humira and Enbrel. In 2014, Abbvies's drug Humira (Adalimumab), a drug that treats rheumatoid arthritis and Crohn's diseases, caused the highest healthcare expenditures in the German market, with € 803.8 million net cost, followed by Pfizer's Enbrel (Etanerept), also treating rheumatoid arthritis and auto immune diseases, with net cost of € 477.5 million (Schwabe 2015: 10). Schwabe (2015: 10), also states that 25 percent of the total pharmaceutical market expenditures in Germany are generated by the 30 highest cost evoking innovative drugs.

2.3 Pharmaceutical Supply Chain

Even though pharmaceutical innovation and production accounts for a sizeable portion of pharmaceutical costs and is therefore used as a justification for high drug prices, only about 66.5 percent of the drugs' market prices are caused by the pharmaceutical company itself. The additional 33.5 percent are raised by pharmacists, wholesalers and taxes (EFPIA 2015: 14). As a consequence, closer attention to the structure of the pharmaceutical market has to be paid, when explaining the reasons for high drug prices and why pharmaceutical firms have an incentive to deter market competition.

The pharmaceutical industry is different to other industries, in the effect that the market it serves, does not only consist of the two typical market sides supply and demand (Chin 2010: 623). Pharmaceutical manufacturers rather face the issue that the person who consumes the good is not the market participant who also pays for the good, as presented in Figure 2.

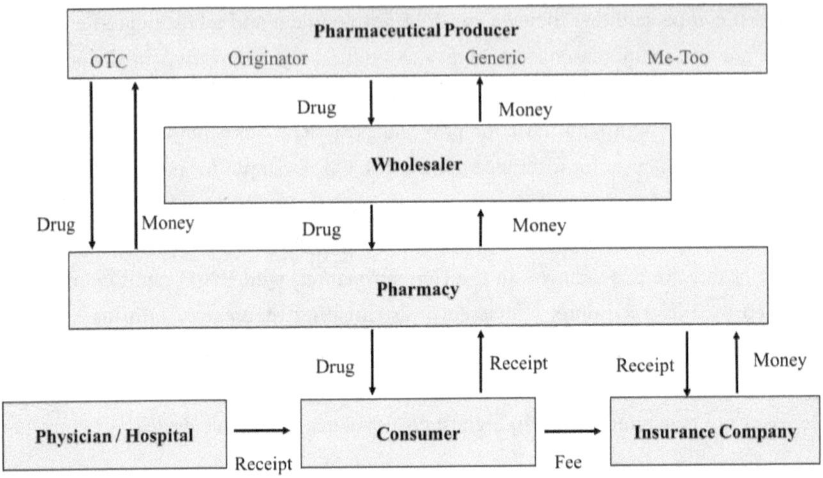

Figure 2: The Pharmaceutical Supply Chain, own representation based on Kanavos and Costa-Font (2005:755), and Pedroso and Nakano 2009: 379.

Usually, insurance companies bear the medical costs, such as paying for medicines.[8] Insurance companies in return negotiate with the producers to get discounts (Pedroso and Nakano 2009: 378; Hosken and Wendling 2013: 187). If there is more than one prescription drug available, containing the same compounds and indication, the insurance company can decide on which drug the patient receives, unless the patients prefer to pay additional cost for another drug out of their own pocket (Puig-Junoy, 2010: 651). Consequently, the demand side is influenced by two participants: the patient who wants to get the best treatment possible and the insurance company that tries to save money by demanding discounts and the cheapest treatment possible.

In addition, consumers demanding the good do not necessarily know their demand and they are not able to directly influence it, respectively (Königbauer 2007: 286). The demand is driven by consumer health. Even if the consumers know what treatment is needed in order to satisfy their demand, they are not allowed to purchase the drug directly from the manufacturer. First, consumers have to reconcile with another market participant, the physician - either in a private practice or at a hospital - who examines the patients and then decides on the right treatment. The physician writes a prescription or directly hands out the drug, if it is an in-patient treatment at a hospital (De Frutosa, Ornaghib and Siotis 2013: 268; Pedroso and Nakano 2009: 378). Consequently, the

8 In the US most insurers, however, also impose so-called "deductibles" where consumers have to pay drugs "out-of-pocked" until they spent a certain amount of money and filled the "deductible". Then the insurer covers the additional spending on drugs (Wharam, Ross-Degnan, and Rosenthal 2013: 1481).

physician is a third market participant who influences the demand side of the traded good by prescribing the active substance (Richard and Van Horn 2004: 525). Hence, there are three market participants that build the demand side of the market.

On the supply side, there are the pharmaceutical companies forming an upstream market. Pharmaceutical companies do not sell their drugs directly to consumers but rather sell them to wholesalers who sell the pharmaceuticals to pharmacists that retail the drugs to end-consumers (Pedroso and Nakano 2009: 378). This is described in more detail later in this chapter and in chapter 3.1. Pharmaceutical companies cannot all be viewed as perfect competitors, because some drugs they are producing are not necessarily homogenous products. This is due to the fact, that there are four different sub-markets within the pharmaceutical market.

One of the sub-markets is the "originator", "brand name" or "pioneer" market. This market includes all products that are new to the market at point of entry and offer some new, innovated treatment of diseases (Bardey, Bommier and Jullien 2010: 304). The name "pioneer" or "originator" drug results from the way of production. These pharmaceuticals are new to the market without any other drug offering the same or similar treatment in the way they do. In most countries, copies of those originator drugs are not allowed to have their own brand name but rather have to display the drug-ingredients. The "original product", in contrast, is allowed to wear a name of own choice. This is why new, patent protected drugs are also referred to as "branded" or "brand name" drugs (Puig-Junoy 2010: 650). All of the products belonging to this market are still or had been patent protected for offering innovative disease treatment. Other firms copy the compound after the patent protection runs out and the first drugs that have similar, or the same ingredients enter the market after the original product's patent has terminated (Gonzalez et al. 2008: 247; Adriaen, De Witte and Simoens 2008: 176). Within the brand name products market there is no direct competition, because all drugs offered are heterogeneous drugs, as their compounds and efficacy are significantly different to other drugs offered in the market (Brekke and Kuhn 2006: 104). Therefore, the original product market can be viewed as monopolistic for every drug offered (Adriaen, De Witte and Simoens 2008: 176).

The second sub-market is the "generic" market. The generic market handles all drugs that are co-substantial to an original product, i.e. they feature the same active substances as originator products both in quantity and quality, without offering any additional benefit of disease treatment in comparison to the branded drug. This means, all drugs without patent protection, and being equipped with the same active ingredients as the brand name drug belong to the market of generics (Scott-Morton 2000: 1086).

Moreover, the generic market is the market that provides competition to the originator products, because it introduces homogenous products that are available for a smaller price, as generic manufacturers did not need to invest in R&D and entry barriers are abolished after patent termination (Puig-Junoy 2010: 650). One modification of generic pharmaceuticals is the so-called "biosimilar" drug. These pharmaceuticals are not bioequivalent copies of originator products, because their active substance contains biological produced proteins rather than chemical entities, that are produced differently to the active ingredients of branded drugs (Schwabe 2015: 25).

Another sub-market is the market for "me-too" drugs. The market for me-too drugs can be viewed as in-between the market for generics and the market for brand name drugs. Me-too drugs are innovative drugs, meaning they are not bioequivalent to branded drugs because they feature compounds or active substances different to the ones fabricated within originator drugs but treat the same disease (Bardey, Bommier and Jullien 2010: 304). Thereupon, they are under patent protection and could be viewed as competitors to original drugs, even though their active substance does not provide an additional benefit to an originator drug that is already available for consumers (Arcidiacono, Ellickson, Landry and Ridley 2013: 538).

The fourth sub-market is the market for Over-the-Counter (OTC) drugs. Those pharmaceuticals are different to the drugs explained above, because the drugs do not need to be prescribed by a physician. In all other sub-markets prescription by a physician is obligatory. The active substance of OTCs is viewed as not causing dangerous damage to the human body, therefore, patients can decide for themselves, if they want to purchase it, without consulting a physician (Guido et al. 2011: 207). This sub-market is the only one where the demand side is formed by patients only. Patients can decide on demand on their own, depending on their willingness to pay only (Bower, Landreth Grau and Taylor 2013: 228).

Even though all the above mentioned sub-markets feature essential differences in the goods they supply, when analyzing the competition issues of the pharmaceutical industry, all those markets can be pooled into one supply market, with only some exceptions concerning the OTC market. As the drugs are not sold directly to consumers, however, the supply side of the pharmaceutical market is divided into an upstream and a downstream-side (Pedroso and Nakano 2009: 378). The pharmaceutical producers represent the upstream market. On the downstream side of the market, there are wholesalers that distribute the drug through pharmacists. In other distribution methods, the pharmaceutical manufacturer sells directly to the pharmacy, but never to the end consumer (Chakrabarti, Ramos and Henneberg 2013: 360). Although pharmacists represent the supply side of the market, they can also influence the demand side. With certain exceptions, in Germany for example, pharmacists are obliged by law to sell the drug with the lowest prices to the consumer, if there is more than one drug with the same active ingredients available (§129 Sozialgesetzbuch (SGB) V). This is also the case in most of the US-States, where pharmacists are allowed to substitute the prescribed originator drug with a cheaper generic drug (Scott-Morton 2000: 1087). Imported pharmaceuticals are handled the same way in Germany. Pharmacists are obliged to sell five percent of their total sales as parallel imported pharmaceuticals to consumers according to §129 SGB V. Therefore, pharmacists can influence consumer's demand, by handing them not necessarily the originator product, consumers might prefer due to risk-aversion and acquaintance with the product, but rather the drug that is cheapest in their stock (Chin 2010: 620; Scott-Morton 2000: 1088).

Since pharmacists and wholesalers have to purchase their stock from the producers and then resell it to the consumers, their only way to generate revenues is by achieving high mark-ups. Since the wholesalers and pharmacies are customers of pharmaceutical manufacturers, their revenues are generated through the difference between the price they pay to the pharmaceutical firm and the price at which the wholesaler sells to the pharmacy and the pharmacy to the end-consumer (Chakrabarti, Ramos and Henneberg 2013: 360).

This is possible by negotiating discounts with the manufacturers, because the prices consumers pay for the product are already set by the regulator and insurance companies that negotiate with the producers, respectively (Adriaen, De Witte and Simoens 2008: 176). As already mentioned above, 33.5 percent of drugs prices are charged by wholesalers, pharmacists and taxes (EFPIA 2015: 14). The higher the discounts, wholesalers get, the higher the mark-up they can charge. In order to achieve those discounts, wholesalers tend to cooperate as purchasing associations to gain a higher market share and buyer power. The more wholesalers build an alliance, the less possibilities a pharmaceutical manufacturer has left to sell its product. Therefore, the manufacturer loses bargaining power and the purchasing cooperation gains bargaining power, which increases the strain of pharmaceutical firms, to set prices high enough in order to be able to grant discounts (Chae and Heidhues 2004: 735). In the US for example, there are only about 20 wholesalers with the three biggest wholesalers covering about 90 percent market share (Jambulingam, Kathuria and Nevin 2009: 306). Garattini, Motterlini, and Cornago (2008: 313), however, claim that these wholesalers' buyer power is limited by regulators that determine the maximum margin a wholesaler is allowed to achieve. Moreover, Fisher Ellison and Snyder, (2010: 32) claim that the

intensity of competition between wholesalers influences their power of demand more intensively, than their market share does.
Consequently, there are five market participants determining the supply and demand side. R&D intensive firms have to generate enough revenues to cover innovation costs due to generic and parallel trade competition as well as bargaining power of downstream firms.

2.4 Different Regulatory Provisions

When analyzing the actions of pharmaceutical market participants that infringe perfect competition, it is also necessary to understand why the pharmaceutical market is different from other markets where goods are sold without any restrictions. One of the main aspects is the fact that the drug industry is a strictly regulated industry. Reference Price Regulation (RPR) and Price Cap Regulation (PCR) are the most commonly used regulation schemes within Europe and the US (Ruggeri and Nolte 2013: 16). Both regulation mechanisms aim to restrict pharmaceutical firms from charging high prices for their drugs, especially while their drug is still patent protected and does not have to face competition.
With PCR, the regulator restricts the drug company's ability from setting the market price for its patented drug higher than a certain maximum price defined by the regulator, i.e. the regulator sets a maximum price that is lower than the price, a profit maximizing firm would set (Brekke, Grasdal and Holmas 2009: 171). RPR, however, is becoming more established in European countries, replacing former PCR in the last decades because it does not restrict the firms in choosing the price for their drugs. Nevertheless, it restricts patients' rates of reimbursement, i.e. the price the insurer reimburses for the drug. Any difference between price for the drug and reimbursement rate has to be paid by the patient. This reimbursement rate is calculated by the regulator based on the price of drugs with similar ingredients that are sold in so-called reference countries (Brekke, Holmas and Straume 2011: 625). Chapter 3.2 will give a detailed overview about different methods of RPR and how pharmaceutical companies use them to prevent competition.
Another aspect, distinguishing the pharmaceutical market from other goods markets is the elasticity of demand of pharmaceutical products. Since prescription drugs are goods that consumers' health is highly dependent on, the demand for prescription drugs is highly inelastic when they are launched on the market (Brekke, Holmas and Straume 2015: 101). Meaning, an increase in prices does not directly affect the quantity demanded by consumers. However, this is only true for a specific group of drugs, displaying certain characteristic.

The elasticity of demand for originator products, for example, usually is inelastic when the drug is launched on the market. Nonetheless, only as long as the drug is patent protected and does not face any competition through other generics, the demand is inelastic (Brekke, Grasdal and Holmas 2009: 170). Ghislandi (2011: 1137) states that, when generic drugs enter the market, competition arises for the brand name product. Generic producers try to undercut originators' prices in order to capture market power, causing the original manufacturer firm to adjust its prices downward. Ghislandi (2011: 1137) as well as Arcidiacono, et al. (2013: 548) affirm that this is because the market entry of generic drugs offers consumers the opportunity to substitute the originator product by a generic drug and receive the same disease treatment for less expenditures, leading to high cross-price elasticities for the generic competitors and the originator product. The elasticity of demand depends on the level of reimbursement determined by the insurance companies. If there is no RPR, the price for a drug is reimbursed in total. Therefore, there exists inelastic demand in the market for drugs with no RPR and reimbursement of the total drug price (Bardey, Bommier and Jullien 2010: 306).

The pharmaceutical industry faces the problem of dynamic demand structures. Manufacturing firms have to adjust their drug's prices to the changing market conditions and simultaneously accommodate those prices to the predefined regulations. As regulation and demand vary in every country, the originator producers face the problem that their incentive is to gain high revenues to cover their cost of production and R&D and simultaneously keep their prices low enough to be able to compete with other low-cost generic companies.

2.5 Overview of Antitrust and Competition Issues in the Pharmaceutical Industry

The facts presented above about the pharmaceutical industry show the complexity of the pharmaceutical market. The cost for innovation of new pharmaceuticals are increasing each year (DiMasi, Hansen, and Grabowski 2003: 162). Knowing that generic market entry reduces their monopoly profits, originator drug manufacturers try to find ways to extend their market exclusivity and deter entry of competitors.

Market complexity can, in this case, help originator producers to thwart competition. Due to interaction of more than one company on the supply side, branded drug manufacturers can circumvent statutory provision and inhibit competition (Carrier 2014: 2). As there exist various ways to influence market entry of possible competitors which can also be used simultaneously to intensify the effect of staving of competition, figure 3 presents an overview that explains all possible ways to deter competition and shows interactions of such ways, I was able to find and analyze during my studies.

This overview gives an indication for chapter 3 and 4, how the anticompetitive actions interact and where they are situated in the market. The figure consists of two countries, 1 and 2. Country 1 is a high price country, where there are two branded drug companies, A and D, and one generic company E. Country 2 is a low price country, where A also supplies its products and there exists another originator drug producer C, and one generic manufacturer B. Parentheses indicate literature I refer to, and brackets show cases I was able to find where producers already used this method of thwarting competition. Each connection line between two manufacturers or a manufacturer and a wholesaler shows a different method for inhibiting competition. All thin broken arrows show the interaction of drug producers with drug distributors, where money is exchanged for the drug.

In order to understand why it is in some cases easier for drug manufacturers to circumvent statutory provisions in the context of the market complexity, the figure shows the supply chain of a drug in a summarized version, as was presented in chapter 2.3. Manufacturer A owns two branches, one in country 1 and one in country 2. Since demand usually differs between those countries and regulatory provisions lead to differences in reimbursement rates, prices vary between those countries. Hence, parallel trade occurs (Valletti 2006: 315). This imposes competition due to arbitrage for producer A, which I will explain in more detail in chapter 3.1. Producer A can, therefore, choose to vertically integrate with a wholesaler, i.e. obtain vertical price control (Birg 2015: 561).

As A is now able to influence parallel distributed drug prices, A is able to compete on the downstream level with parallel traded drugs and can secure market shares and prevent profit losses. In addition to that, producer A can align prices in the two countries (Danzon, Mulcahy, and Towse 2015: 240). This convergence of prices reduces the margin of wholesalers, preventing them from performing arbitrage. In this case prices do not have to be exactly equal in both countries due to transaction costs of parallel trade (Bart 2008: 999). Hence producers are still able to perform a version of price discrimination. Another possibility to deter competition by parallel trade is to change the product in one of the two countries to achieve a difference between the offered drugs. In this case, producer A offers the same pharmaceutical in both markets but different administration forms. If there are differences in market approved administration forms drugs cannot be imported. For that reason, parallel trade is not possible (Moore and Montagnon 2010: 688).

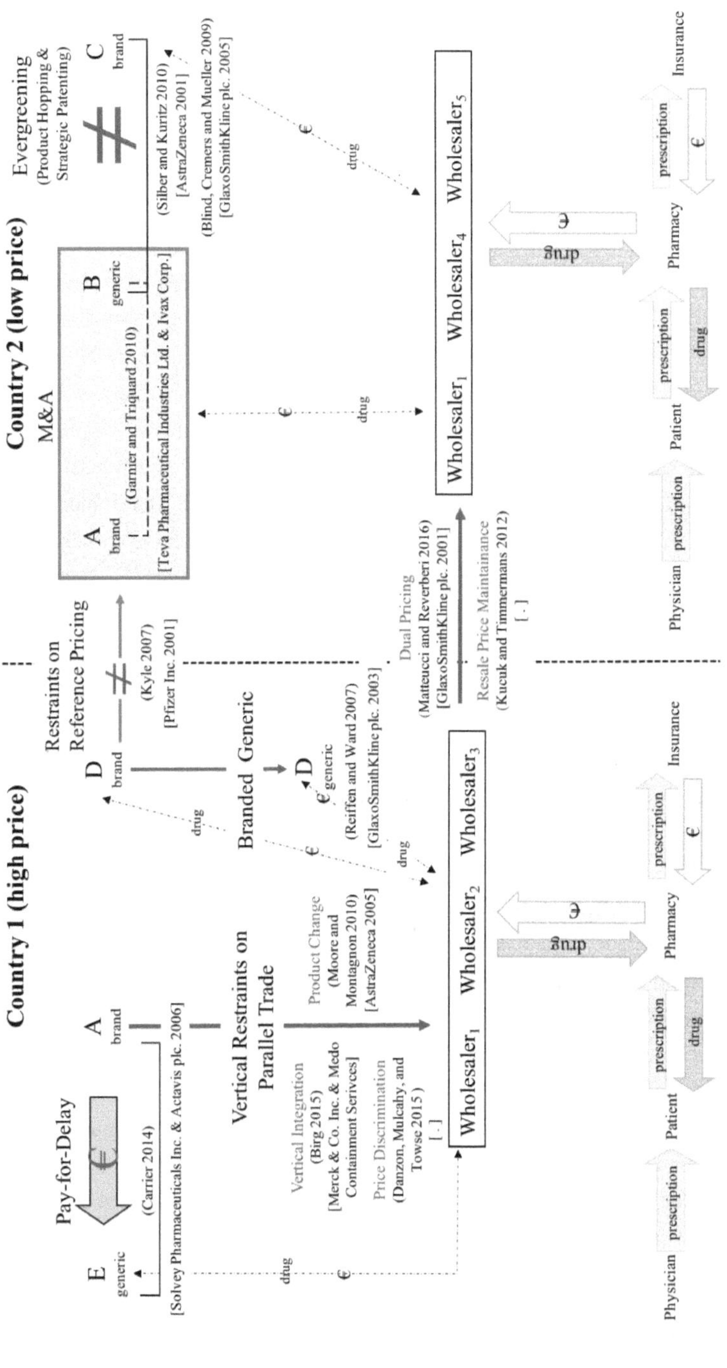

Figure 3: Model of Antitrust and Competition Violation in the Pharmaceutical Industry, own representation

If a change of the drugs administration form is not feasible, manufacturer A can alternatively induce a price floor, where wholesalers are obliged to sell the drug at the retail level for the price, the manufacturer induced. This is also called Resale Price Maintenance (RPM). It helps branded drug producer A to influence the price at retail level and ensures that parallel traded drugs are not sold at a lower price than the drug produced in the country of origin (Kucuk and Timmermans 2012: 537). As RPM often violates competition law and is only applicable in some exceptions, there is another way to prevent parallel trade. Producer A, can induce so-called “dual pricing”. In this case A sells the drug for a higher price to wholesalers in country 1 that want to export the drug to country 2. With this, firm A ensures that the distributors’ margins become low and they have less incentive to perform parallel trade (Matteucci and Reverberi 2016: 51).

Along with parallel trade reducing profits of originator drug manufacturers, regulatory provisions can reduce drug prices and lead to a reduction in profits of brand name drug manufacturers. Especially external reference pricing, which is analyzed in more detail in chapter 3.2, induces competition to patent protected drugs as reimbursement rates are calculated with reference to similar pharmaceuticals in other countries (Valletti 2006: 315). Since prices for similar treatments vary across countries 1 and 2, drug producer D can circumvent lower reimbursement levels when not launching the drug in the lower price country 2. This is due to the fact, that there is no lower price, regulators can refer to when choosing a regulating scheme based on external reference pricing (Kyle 2007: 88).

Parallel trade and regulatory provisions, however, are not the only cases that induce competition to a branded drug. After patent termination, generic entry leads to competition. This competition does not only reduce prices but also takes away branded drug producer D’s market shares. Therefore, D’s profits decrease as firm D has to reduce prices and is not able to serve the whole demand (Grabowski and Kyle, 2007). Firm D can prevent significant losses of market shares by producing an own generic drug called “branded generic”. Manufacturer D sells the branded generic when D observes other generic drugs entering the market. This does not totally deter generic competition, but reduces profit losses, as D is able to compete with a generic product (Reiffen and Ward 2007: 254). Another form of generic competition deterrence is performed by brand name firm C in country 2. This action is the so-called “Evergreening”, where additional patents are filed for a changed product (product hopping) or a changed indication (Extending Indication Approval). The generic competitor B is then only able to offer a substitute for one product version and C can serve the whole market with the enhanced product versions (Hemphill and Sampat 2012: 328; Silber and Kuritz 2010: 121; Blind, Cremers, and Mueller 2009: 428).

In addition to these actions, where only one firm deters competition, there are interactions between generic and branded drug producers to delay competition after patent termination. One of these actions is the "pay for delay" agreement. In the case of pay for delay, firm A, settled in country 1, pays firm E a certain amount of money. In exchange for the transaction, firm E delays its market entry by a specified amount of time that A determines. In some cases, this pay for delay happens related to product hopping or launch of branded generics, which will be explained further in chapter 4.1. (Carrier 2014: 6)

In contrast to pay for delay, where both companies only agree on a certain action, there exists the cooperation of a branded and generic drug manufacturer. This is the so-called Merger and Acquisition, where both firms build a new firm which is performed in country 2, where the branded drug manufacturer mergers with (or acquires) the generic manufacturer (Garnier and Trinquard 2010). In this case the branded drug producer cannot only hinder the generic producer from launching the drug on the market but is also able to produce branded generics cheaply, as explained in chapter 4.2 (Cefis and Marsili 2015: 699). Figure 3, thus, gives an overview over the pharmaceutical industry, including actions branded manufactures can perform to weaken, delay or deter entry of competitors.

3. Anticompetitive actions taken by one firm only

Since branded drug companies lose market shares and monopoly profits when competitors enter, innovators tend to prevent competition to extend their monopoly power. As Bennato and Valletti (2014: 83) claim in their paper, monopoly power is gained through patent protection. Correspondingly, it is especially in the interest of originator companies to keep their monopoly power by extending patent protection and detain competition. Even before patent termination, however, parallel trade can induce competition for branded drug producers (Graslandt and Maskus 2004: 1036). Vertical restraints are therefore implemented by producers to reduce parallel trade competition. In addition to that, there are several possibilities to thwart generic competition, also performed by the branded manufacturer only. In this chapter I will present anticompetitive actions performed by branded drug producers only.

3.1 Vertical Restraints under Parallel Trade

Trigger for competition that arises during patent protection are parallel imported drugs. This is why I will first present features about parallel trade and why it can lead to competition for branded originators, before I examine possibilities to restrain parallel trade. Parallel imports in the pharmaceutical industry are pharmaceuticals produced and supplied in one country and then exported to another country. This trade of drugs specializes mainly on originator drugs that are still patent protected. Wholesalers headquartered in one country purchase patented prescription drugs in another country and then resell them in their home country (Li and Maskus 2006: 433). These downstream distributors have to acquire licenses that allow them to resell the parallel traded drug in the destination country (Kanavos and Vandoros 2010: 325).

Health insurance companies bargain about reimbursement rates with drug developing firms in every country. This leads to diverse reimbursement levels for the same drugs. Moreover, there are different regulation models in every country, leading to different maximum prices a company can charge for its drugs (Grossman and Lai 2008: 379; Raff and Schmitt 2007: 436). Pharmaceutical manufacturers try to implement third degree price discrimination in order to capture consumers' surpluses in every country (Jelovac and Bordoy 2005: 6).

As pharmaceutical manufacturers are not allowed to sell their products directly to the end consumer, but rather through different distributors, their influence on the supply chain of their product is relatively small (Kanavos and Vandoros 2010: 326). Hence, it is possible for wholesalers to purchase the drugs from the producing firm, at a market where the price for the drug is relatively low compared to other markets. Without a permission of the manufacturing company, distributors are allowed to resell the drugs on a market where prices for patented drugs are relatively high, compared to the market of origin, if the manufacturing firm is active on both markets, offering the same good (Li and Maskus 2006: 443). Parallel distributors can perform arbitrage and level out price differences between countries arisen through third degree price discrimination. This arbitrage is legitimated in the EU by the European Court of Justice and in the US by state governments. Especially the unrestricted movement of goods within the EU, secured through the European Single Market, allows for this arbitrage according to the Treaty on the Functioning of the European Union (TFEU) Article 28. In the US, drugs are allowed to be reimported by distributers according to the FDA based on 21 U.S.C. §381 (d).

Jelovac and Bordoy (2005: 7) conclude in their paper that arbitrage does not directly cause a uniform price for both countries, but induces aligned prices in the parallel traded countries. In addition to that, the price elasticities of demand vary between parallel traded markets since there exists differences in price regulation. Different need for treatments influences this difference in the elasticity of demand. The treatment of endemic diseases especially, leads to variation in demand. Demand for endemic diseases is more elastic in regions, where the disease does not often occur, in comparison to areas where the disease is common. As the World Health Organization (WHO) (2016) claims, demand for typhus vacancies is relatively low in central Europe and northern America compared to demand in Asia, central Africa and southern America where typhus is endemic. This creates a more inelastic demand in southern Africa and Asia and a relatively elastic demand in Europe and the US and allows for price differences between those regions.

Moreover, consumers might observe parallel traded drugs as qualitatively less valuable, because of different packaging or labelling. Thus, demand for those parallel traded drugs is more elastic than for the original product. Resulting from this, parallel distributors might not be able to compensate third degree price discrimination in total, leaving manufacturers some proportion of price differentiation (Birg 2015: 561; Matteucci and Reverberi 2016: 51).

Even though each country has its own law regarding labelling and re-packaging of parallel traded pharmaceuticals, most of them imply that consumers have to be able to identify parallel traded drugs as drugs originally produced for another country (Duso, Herr, and Suppliet 2014: 1037). Thus, parallel distributors face the cost of re-packaging and labelling plus the cost of shipping the drugs from one country to another in addition to the purchasing price for the drug. Therefore, total costs of distributors have to be smaller than the cost a distributor faces for purchasing and reselling in a country with high drug prices, in order for parallel trade to be attractive (Li and Maskus 2006: 446). Consequently, there are higher shares of parallel traded pharmaceuticals in countries where prices for drugs are relatively high, such as Germany and Sweden in comparison to other European countries (Kanavos and Costa-Font 2005: 754).

The effect of parallel trade on competition is often discussed by economists. Even as Kanavos and Vandoros (2010: 336) conclude that parallel trade does not necessarily lead to price competition, Duso, Herr, and Suppliet (2014: 1036) find that allowing for arbitrage leads to reduced prices of patented drugs. In order to be able to compete with the prices of their parallel imported products, manufacturers have to reduce the market price, reducing expenses for healthcare providers. Hence, even the fear of parallel traded pharmaceuticals entering the market can lead drug producers to lower their drug prices (Li and Robles 2007: 417). As a consequence, revenues decrease and profits of R&D intensive drug manufacturers will fall. This reduces the incentive to innovate with the amount of parallel imported drugs entering the market (Li and Maskus 2006: 445).

Along with that, Jelovac and Bordoy (2005: 7) ascertain that parallel trade influences welfare negatively. Welfare decreases, if countries with no difference in need for drugs and only varying in reimbursement levels face parallel trade. This is because consumers value the drug the same in both countries and supply is shifted to the country with higher reimbursement level. On the other hand, as needs for medication differ across countries, parallel trade can allocate drugs to the markets with the greater need and higher willingness to pay, increasing allocative efficiency. If the demand for the drug is more elastic in low price countries than in high price countries and both countries face the same regulation, parallel trade ensures that consumers with greater need for the drug, get the drug for a lower price (Jelovac and Bordoy 2005: 17). There are differences in findings concerning increase of competition through parallel trade. Those differences, however, occur as the literature I examined only studies price changes after parallel trade occurred. Literature, therefore, does not consider anticompetitive actions of branded companies which I present later in this chapter. Li and Maskus (2006: 444) claim that due to parallel trade originator manufacturers experienced about $ 3 billion profit reduction each year. Thus, it is in the producers' interest to prevent competition and keep their market power, gained through IPR protection, until generic competition arises. Consequently, it needs to be examined how originator pharmaceutical producers are able to prevent competition that occurs through parallel imports.

3.1.1 Vertical Integration

As already stated above, manufacturing companies are not able to influence the distribution of their goods directly. This is the reason, why wholesalers are able to perform parallel trade (Kanavos and Vandoros 2010: 326). If parallel trade occurs, monopolists are not able to build barriers to market entry, even if they are protected from generic entry through patents. Exhaustion of IPR withdraws manufacturers' rights to decide on destination of product selling (Grossman and Lai 2008: 379). In addition to that, a reduction of monopoly prices might not deter market entry of parallel imports effectively (Birg 2015: 559). Therefore, manufacturers need to expand their influence on the supply chain of their product, in order to control the distribution way of their product and compete with parallel traded drugs (Graslandt and Maskus 2007: 945). Since producers are dependent on wholesalers as downstream distributors of their product, they can choose vertical integration (VI) as a solution to gain higher influence on the distribution ways of their product (Chen and Maskus 2005: 13).

VI occurs when two companies at different vertical levels, within the process of value creation of a good, agree on integrating their development process by forming a contract or directly merging. Because both companies are situated at different levels of the product's distribution chain, they do not compete, as it would be the case with horizontal integration (Simonet 2007 a: 144). Even when both firms take part in the supply chain of the good, there is no need for both firms to create new output. The upstream manufacturer can either produce an intermediate good, which is sold to a downstream company where additional input is added and the product is changed before it is sold to the consumer. However, the upstream firm can also cover the whole production process and sell the final good to the downstream company that only undertakes the function of supplying the good (Perry, 1988). As pharmaceutical producers have to retail their good through wholesalers who do not have influence on the production process of the drug, as shown in figure 2, I will refer to VI as the upstream manufacturer taking care of the whole production process and the wholesaler on the downstream level only fulfilling the task of supplying the product.

Through VI, producers can generate additional knowledge about consumers' preferences since they directly interact with retailers. Moreover, they are able to decide which distributors to serve, excluding distributors that represent the greatest threat to monopoly power (Simonet 2007: 19). Additionally, VI reduces transaction costs for the integrated firm. Acemoglu, Johnson, and Mitton (2009: 1251) state that transaction costs for nonintegrated firms are higher than for integrated firms if their relationship in trade is examined for long-term interaction. The producer has to pay higher transaction costs to prevent the distributor from reimporting the drug to another country if they are not integrated. With VI there is no need for this incentive payment. Furthermore, there are no bargaining cost after contracts are settled, because integrated distributors do not need to bargain for discounts as their interests in profits are aligned with the branded manufacturer's profit interest (Acemoglu, Johnson, and Mitton 2009: 1251). This, consequently, can reduce drug expenditures for insurance companies, if the reduction in transaction costs is passed on to the consumer (Chen and Maskus 2005: 4). Due to VI, double marginalization is eliminated. The integrated manufacturer is able to sell the drug to a price lower than other wholesalers, because the VI company does not face transaction costs for purchasing the good from the manufacturer. The integrated company attains cost-advantages to other non-integrated distributors and the producer can retain high market prices (Simonet 2007: 20). However, Birg, (2015: 546) analyzes the effect of parallel trade on VI and proves that double marginalization is only omitted if parallel trade does not exist. If parallel trade occurs, drug manufacturers will impose double mark-ups in order to keep other distributors out of the market. Her justification for her findings is that, due to low wholesale prices, possible entrants are attracted to the market. The higher the wholesale price is, the less distributors are attracted to enter. The integrated company has no need to generate revenues on downstream levels and is therefore able to compete for lower market prices by being able to decrease the prices at the downstream level (Birg 2015: 546). In addition to that, foreclosure effects of VI can raise costs for other non-integrated distributors. If the producer is able to secure strategically valuable market outlets, other distributors will not be able to access low cost outlets and need to raise the retail price of the drug. In this case, the manufacturer is able to gain price advantages, even if double marginalization is not omitted (Lafontaine and Slade 2007: 664).

Furthermore, integrated distributors are able to gain access to valuable resources and market outlets because of cooperation with the producer. Even if manufacturers are not able to deter other distributors from parallel trading the original drug, they can decrease profits of other downstream companies through foreclosure of strategic resources and market outlets. Since producers are able to observe information about consumers' preferences more closely through the integrated downstream firm they adjust the drug to the consumers' preferences and gain more brand loyalty (Simonet 2007 a: 145). As already stated above, parallel imported drugs might be observed as lower in quality by consumers. Also integrated distributors already have access to packaging machinery of the manufacturers, leading to cost efficiency (Birg 2015: 558). They, therefore, have the advantage to produce a reimported drug that is observed qualitatively equal to the original product but observed higher in quality in comparison to other parallel imports, by consumers (Matteucci and Reverberi 2016: 51). Consequently, VI of producer and distributor can deter other distributors from entering the market by establishing barriers to entry.

Although VI can reduce costs of originator manufacturers and help to prevent distributors from re-importing the drug and imposing price competition, there are costs that occur to the manufacturer when integrating. Those costs can be seen as another form of transaction costs (Acemoglu, Johnson, and Mitton 2009: 1252). The downstream distributor, who now shares goals with the producer still needs to be monitored by the upstream manufacturer. Producers have to secure that the distributor satisfies contract obligations and maximizes efficiency (Simonet 2007: 21). Acemoglu, Johnson, and Mitton (2009: 1265) refer to this as cost of monitoring, where the upstream firm as principal has to set incentives for the downstream firm as agent, to act in favor of the profit maximizing producer. Hence, costs for VI have to be smaller, than the losses the manufacturer faces when parallel trade occurs.

Acemoglu, Johnson, and Mitton (2009: 1252-1256) analyze this possibility more closely in their paper. They consider, that integration creates interest payments, since the integrating firm might need to acquire debt for absorbing the downstream company. Also they assume market imperfection leading to interest payments for the manufacturer, meaning that the transaction costs for integration reduce profits not only by one unit for each unit of transaction but also by some discount factor δ. Therefore, their profit from integrating π_{VI} minus the discounted transaction costs $(1+\delta)t$ has to be greater than the profit the manufacturer earns without vertically integrating π_M.

$$\pi_{VI} - (1+\delta)t \geq \pi_M \tag{3.1}$$

Another key aspect concerning the ability of downstream integrated drug producers to perform parallel trade is the legal aspect. European law limits the abilities of pharmaceutical manufacturers to perform anticompetitive actions. Article 101 (1) TFEU says that integrated firms are not allowed to perform actions that directly restrict competition and free trade within the European Single Market. In the case of restricting parallel trade through VI, this means that the integrated manufacturer is not allowed to exclude other distributors from accessing the products. Although, article 101 (3) TFEU allows the constraint of competition through integration if the firm performing anti-competitive actions can verify that the efficiency gain of this action outweigh the efficiency losses of anti-competitive actions. Along with that Article 102 (c) TFEU forbids any action taken by a firm to abuse its dominant market position. In the above mentioned case, this would limit the manufacturers abilities to use their market-dominating position, they would achieve through VI, because of cost advantages over other distributors. This is why the manufacturer might limit parallel trade but is not able to detain it in total because it offends article 101 TFEU.

Similar to the European law, there are statutory provisions in the US-American law that limit companies' abilities to thwart competition. One of those statutory provisions is Section 3 of the Clayton Act. It prohibits trade arrangements that lead to exclusively serving one distributor and discriminates other distributors as it negatively influences competition and free trade (15 U.S.C. §14). In addition to that, Clayton Act Section 7 prohibits any integration of two companies that creates monopolies or restricts competition (15 U.S.C. §18). This is consistent with Section 2 of the Sherman Act prohibiting any arrangements between firms that lead to monopoly power of those firms (15 U.S.C. §2). However, Section 5 of the Federal Trade Commission (FTC) Act limits the above mentioned prohibitions as it allows anticompetitive restrictions if the social benefits of those actions outweigh the social losses and consumers are not harmed (15 U.S.C. §45). This is similar to the European law and also known as the "rule of reason". If the benefit from anti-competitive actions outweigh the societies losses of that action, the per-se rule which forbids any anti-competitive action is suspended and violation of law has to be decided on a case-by-case basis.

An example for such VI of a manufacturer and a distributor in the pharmaceutical market is the case of Merck's integration with the Pharmaceutical Business Managers (PBM) company Medco Containment Services. PBMs are market participants that bargain with drug producers about discounts for consumers and insurers, and observe prescription behaviors of physicians and information about consumers. They also operate as distributor between manufacturer and pharmacy (Simonet 2007: 22). As Simonet (2007 a: 144) states in his paper, in 1993 the pharmaceutical company Merck invested $ 6.6 billion to integrate with the US company Medco Containment Services which was one of the largest PBM companies back then. Similar VIs could be observed at the end of the 1990s. The goal was to acquire control over the drug distribution process and to be able to design a more efficient R&D process due to information about consumers' preferences gained through the PBMs. This should minimize total cost and increase profits due to early market entry (Simonet 2007: 26). Simonet (2007: 28) concludes also, that the integrated manufacturers could use their power over distribution channels to justify price differences between competitor products and the original drug.

This intensification of VI in the 1990s, declined in the last two decades as the benefit of achieving intensified control over distribution processes was outrun by the costs and legal barriers. High transaction costs occurred for acquiring the downstream companies and profits did not increase significantly. Hence, most of the integrations were reversed in the 2000s, creating losses for the manufactures instead of additional profits. Moreover, investments in VI reduced manufacturers' abilities to implement R&D because the assets spent on integrating could have been invested in R&D (Simonet 2007 a: 153).

Although the above mentioned cases do not directly contribute to reimporting patent protected drugs, they give an overview about what a manufacturer has to consider, when vertically integrating with a distributor, such as cost for integration and monitoring in combination with profits as well as legal aspects. VI can lead to producers' cost-advantages over distributors and therefore help them to weaken competition at the downstream level. In addition to that, it can help the manufacturer prevent parallel trade and loss of market shares. However, it constitutes new costs for acquiring downstream firms and monitoring compliance of new company parts. Along with that, the manufacturer has to consider legal boundaries. Correspondingly, the drug producer has to weigh the cost for VI against the benefit of preventing parallel imports and keeping a dominant market position.

Since originator manufacturers only have a limited amount of time to generate profits that cover their innovation cost and acquire savings to invest in new innovation, it is necessary for those innovators to deter competition as long as possible. As parallel trade threatens this profit maximization, manufacturers try to prevent this parallel trade. Integrating vertically is one possibility to do so and therefore, should be analyzed more closely in the future.

3.1.2 Price Discrimination

Apart from VI there are additional actions to prevent competition caused by parallel trade which have to be analyzed. Birg (2015: 558) examines that parallel trade influences drug prices in both countries subject to parallel trade and allows for arbitrage. Due to parallel trade, pricing decisions in both countries are linked to each other. Hence, differences in prices are no longer feasible as price discrimination can be averted by distributors. According to Birg (2015: 560), this parallel trade causes manufacturers to adjusts prices of the parallel traded countries in order to reduce the distributors' abilities to perform arbitrage. Originator manufacturers either raise the prices in the low-price country or reduces the price in the high price country (Danzon, Mulcahy, and Towse 2015: 240). The ability of adjustment, nevertheless, depends on the regulation restrictions in each country. While there are differences in the regulation of prices between the countries, maximum chargeable prices vary across countries. Regulators only reimburse those maximum prices and consumers have to pay any additional cost out of pocket. As consumers' willingness to pay differs across countries, various maximum prices arise. To price discriminate in each country, originator producers set the maximum price they are able to charge in order realize maximum profits possible (Bennato and Valletti 2014: 83; Kyle, Allsbrook, and Schulman 2008: 1308). If parallel trade occurs, manufacturers are not able to raise the price in the low-price country further, as they are already charging the maximum prices. This is why they can only reduce prices charged in the high-price countries in order to prevent arbitrage (Kyle, Allsbrook, and Schulman 2008: 1310). This is consistent with the findings of Guo, Hu, and Zhong (2013: 346), stating that parallel trade decreases prices of drugs.

While, due to brand loyalty, consumers observe parallel traded drugs to be lower in quality in comparison to the original product and therefore as an imperfect substitute, the price of the original product does not have to be perfectly equal to the parallel traded drugs (Birg 2015: 561). The price of the branded drug only has to be small enough for the parallel distributor to not generate any profits from reselling the good in the high-price country, leaving the manufacturer the possibility to price discriminate between both countries to a certain extent. As Jelovac and Bordoy (2005: 14) claim, parallel trade does not necessarily lead to uniform prices, but rather convergence of prices between two countries.

Similar to the case of vertical integration, however, legal boundaries have to be considered when deciding to price discriminate by adjusting prices. In the presented case, the manufacturer obtaining a monopoly position in the upstream market can exploit this dominant market position in order to deter competition. In the EU as well as in the US, exploiting monopoly position, nevertheless is forbidden, as it violates Article 102 TFEU and Sherman Act Section 1 and 2 (15 U.S.C §1-2). US law, on the other hand, is less strict, as it prohibits the restriction of free trade through monopoly abuse according to 15 U.S.C §1. Since the convergence of prices does not directly prevent distributors from performing parallel trade, a per se illegality does not exist. After producers reduce prices for their drug in high price countries, parallel distributors are not able to generate significant margins when parallel trading drugs. Distributors can set the prices for parallel traded drugs maximally just beneath the price of originator drugs as the willingness to pay of consumers is lower for parallel traded drugs. Hence, the more converged prices are, the lower the possible margin for downstream distributors is. If manufacturers set prices for their drugs low enough for distributors to not be able to cover transportation cost, distributors will not serve the market (Bart 2008: 999).

Nonetheless, even if there exists a violation of Article 102 TFEU and Sherman Act Section 1 and 2, price adjustment by manufacturers do not affect consumers' surplus directly. While prices are reduced by the manufacturer in the high price country, the demand side has to pay less for the original product than they had to pay before price reduction. Therefore, consumers can afford the original product for the same money they pay for the imperfect parallel traded substitute. Consequently, they are able to obtain the higher quality product for the price of the lower quality product. In this case FTC Act Section 5 (15 U.S.C § 45), in the US, and article 101 (3) TFEU can be applied as social benefits might outweigh social cost. Thus, the rule of reason can be applied for parallel trade cases where prices are adjusted by manufacturers, to examine, whether the effects of price convergence on welfare outweigh the anti-competitive effects.

Hence, an alignment of prices in both countries and performance of arbitrage on their own is another possibility for originator drug manufacturers to weaken parallel trade. In that case prices are either increased in low-price countries or decreased in high price countries. With this action, price differences between both countries are diminished. Convergence of prices leads to manufacturers performing arbitrage where distributors have no incentive to reimport drugs from low-price countries, as they are not able to achieve profitable mark-ups (Bang and Jin 2015: 9). This form of staving off competition is not per se violating antitrust and competition law in the US and EU and therefore can be a legal and effective way to thwart competition through parallel trade. As it is in originator manufacturers' interest to maximize profits, on the other hand, implementing the price alignment can reduce their incentive to invest in innovation and deter them from performing R&D in the future.

3.1.3 Resale Price Maintenance

Adjusting prices in two countries, to diminish price differences is one possibility to prevent parallel trade as it takes away distributor's ability to generate profit. Like shown above, this can deter distributors from arbitraging as long as price differences between the two countries are small enough to prevent distributors from generating profits (Bart 2008: 999). However, if parallel trade is sufficiently prevented, manufacturers need to increase their prices in high-price countries again to generate monopoly profits. This attracts downstream distributors to perform arbitrage. Therefore, the only option of manufacturers is to keep prices in high (low) -price countries efficiently low (high) to prevent parallel trade (Danzon, Mulcahy, and Towse 2015: 340). As price alignments lead to profit reductions for manufacturers in the long run, producers try to find additional possibilities to prevent parallel imports from entering the market in high-price countries.

Another way using vertical restraints to reduce parallel trade is the so-called "Resale Price Maintenance" (RPM). The concept of RPM lets an upstream firm influence a downstream distributor to keep distribution prices at a certain price floor and not undercut this predefined price level by dictating price floors or agreeing on a fixed price (Giovannetti and Magazzini 2013: F582). This means that originator manufacturers can determine the price at which their product is retailed at the downstream level to customers (Mathewson and Winter 1998: 58). Through this vertical price control, manufacturers can influence parallel traders pricing mechanisms to the way that distributors are not setting their prices in high price countries beneath the price for the branded drug.

Even though this restrains distributors' abilities to influence the market price, it allows distributors to achieve a fixed revenue without price competition between distributors (Bang and Jin 2015: 1). With all parallel imports being substitutable, the competition between parallel traders leads to Bertrand competition on prices where all parallel distributors are competing by undercutting their prices (Vandoros and Kanavos 2014: 857). Under RPM, however, those distributors are not competing for prices but only for market shares through quantity and quality differences (Kucuk and Timmermans 2012: 540). Their prices can exceed marginal cost leaving them mark-ups to generate profits. With RPM manufacturers are able to determine both, the wholesale and retail prices for their drugs. Manufacturers predefine the price on retail level at some price floor equal to the price for the original product. Hence, distributors are able to generate profits if they choose the profit maximizing quantity (Wang 2004: 400). Thus, distributors do not necessarily suffer directly from RPM and manufacturers directly benefit, as distributors are able to set prices above their marginal cost (Bonett and Dubois 2010: 156; Rey and Vergé 2010: 952). Moreover, manufacturers can generate significantly higher profits again, because there is no price competition anymore.

Regarding the legal framework in the US and EU, RPM was long considered as violating statuary provisions that protect competition and therefore being illegal, regardless of welfare effects (Wang 2004: 390). In the precedent of Dr. Miles Medical Co. v. John D. Park & Sons[9] the US Supreme Court ruled RPM to be per se illegal[10]. Manufacturers setting price floors, i.e. minimal prices the distributor has to charge for the product, can be linked to price fixing where companies agree on setting the same prices, which is also not allowed by competition law as it limits free trade (Foros, Kind, and Shaffer 2011: 179; Kucuk and Timmermans, 2012: 538). The effect for total welfare, indeed,

9 In 1911 the medical company Dr. Miles Medical imposed price floors for their products on retail level to signal high quality products through high prices. The Supreme Court, however, did not allow this RPM as it was found to be per se violating Sherman Act Section 1 (Moloshok 2007: 13).

10 See US Supreme Court (1911) 'Dr. Miles Medical Co. v. John D. Park & Sons 220 U.S. 373 (1911)', *Certiorari to the Circuit of Appeals for the Sixth Circuit,* URL: https://goo.gl/ROjPVR (retrieved May 10, 2016).

depends on the extent to which RPM influences retail prices upward, leading to increased total cost for consumers (Jullien and Rey 2007: 984). Consequently, claiming RPM to be per se illegal had to be revisited, in case the RPM helps innovating companies to gain enough profits to cover development cost, through restricting parallel trade, without affecting total welfare.

Over the last decades, exceptions to the violation of law were made and rule of reason approaches were performed. An example for such exceptions is in the German book market. Price floors are allowed there, as an exception from Article 101 TFEU (Kucuk and Timmermans 2012: 539). After the U.S Supreme Court ruled RPM to be per se illegal, it did relax the legal framework for RPM in 1919 with the so-called "Colgate doctrine" (Wang 2004: 330). This doctrine allowed manufacturers to set fixed retail prices and not serve distributors that refuse to set these predefined prices. Nevertheless, the doctrine was restricted to that point, that the RPM was no outcome of collusive behavior between distributor and manufacturer but rather be decided by the manufacturer on their own (U.S. Supreme Court 1919[11]). According to this doctrine, RPM was not per se illegal anymore. Rule of reason approaches, yet, were not directly applied in the RPM context until 2006, where the US Supreme Court's decision on RPM as being per se illegal was finally overthrown (Jullien and Rey 2007: 983). In another case, the Supreme Court decided on abandoning the U.S. Supreme Court's decision of 1919[10] and officially claimed RPM and other vertical restrictions to be evaluated according to rule of reason standards (U.S. Supreme Court 2006[12]).

In the EU, similar to the US, vertical restraints including RPM were primarily seen as deterring competition and therefore violating competition regulations set in Art. 101 TFEU. However, this Article only prohibits vertical restraints that limit free trade, if two firms agree on those restraining actions, indirectly allowing RPM where no collusion behavior is verifiable. This is similar to the US Colgate doctrine, leaving a loophole for manufacturers that exert RPM unilaterally. Hence RPM actions do not per se violate EU competition law, but also have to be analyzed according to rule of reason approaches (Kucuk and Timmermans 2012: 539). Moreover, the EU law differentiates between RPM inducing maximum retail prices and minimum retail prices. The case of maximum retail prices, also referred to as price ceiling is ruled less strictly, than minimum prices, as shown in the example of German book market, where such a price fixing is

11 See U.S. Supreme Court (1919) 'United States v. Colgate & Co. 250 U.S. 300 (1919)'*Error to the District Court of the United States for the Eastern District of Virgina,* URL: https://goo.gl/xSsJwT (retrieved May 11, 2016).

12 See U.S. Supreme Court (2006), 'Leegin Creative Leather Products Inc. v. PSKS Inc. No. 06-480', *Certiorari to the United States Court of Appeals for the fifth Circuit*, URL: http://goo.gl/5CbUfu (retrieved May 10, 2016).

permitted[13] (Jullien and Rey 2007: 983; Kucuk and Timmermans 2012: 539). In addition to that, the European Commission instituted a regulation to determine whether a vertical restraint violates Article 101 TFEU or not. With the implementation of a regulation in 2010, the European Commission ruled that all vertical restrictions being implemented by companies covering a market share of less or equal to 30% are permissible, independent of efficiency outcomes. Still, there are some vertical restrictions that fall under "hardcore restrictions" meaning no exception from per se rule is applicable. RPM counts to those "hardcore restrictions" if they cover more than 50% market share (European Commission 2010[14], Art. 4 and 6). If resale prices are recommended by the manufacturer and not mandatory for distributors, Art. 4 of this regulation does not apply and RPM is applicable (Kucuk and Timmermans 2012: 593).

It can be said that RPM offers pharmaceutical manufacturers the possibility to gain more control over the distribution process of their drug and its prices. Consequently, producers achieve greater control over possible competition because of being able to influence all retail prices. RPM, notwithstanding, is an illegal action punished in the EU and US in most cases which causes manufacturers to search for loopholes in law to perform RPM.

3.1.4 Product Change

RPM and price adjustments between countries are two possibilities to thwart parallel trade competition. However, originator manufacturers found an additional action of vertical restraint to inhibit parallel trade competition. This possibility concerns an alteration of products that are subject to parallel trade.

The European Commission ruled that parallel traded drugs must contain the same active substance and administration form, as well as effectiveness for the patient, as the originator drug, sold in the country of destination (Commission of the European Communities: 19[15]). Since parallel traded drugs have to be almost identical to the drugs manufactured in the country they are imported to, a change of administration form can prevent distributors from being able to export the drug into another country (Graslandt and Maskus 2004: 1038). Resulting from this, the manufacturing producer can register patent rights for different administration forms of their products in different countries.

---

13 Note that in this special case prices are not allowed to be higher than the fixed price but also not to be lower.

14 See European Commission (2010), 'Regulation (EU) No 330/2010', *Official Journal of the European Union L 102/1-7,* URL: http://goo.gl/dS648 (retrieved May 10, 2016).

15 See Commission of the European Communities (2003), 'Communication (COM) /2003/839 - Final Commission Communication on Parallel Imports of Proprietary Medicinal Products for Which Marketing Authorisations have Already Been Granted', *Communication from the Commission*, URL: http://goo.gl/HzhTYi (retrieved May 09, 2016).

An example for this change of administration form is the case of AstraZeneca's drug Prilosec (former called Losec, but amended in 1990). AstraZeneca sold Prilosec (omeprazole), a drug to treat gastric ulcer, in several EU countries. Facing the threat of parallel trade and therefore competition, the producer removed the patent registration for the administration form of capsules in three EU member states. The deregistration concerned Norway, Sweden and Denmark (Moore and Montagnon 2010: 688). Since Prilosec capsules were not registered in those markets anymore, parallel distributors were not allowed to sell parallel imported Prilosec capsules in those countries. In addition to competition through parallel trade, AstraZeneca faced the threat of generic market entry as their patent for Prilosec was about to expire. Generic competitors applied for market entry of generics Prilosec capsules versions. Due to deregistration of Prilosec capsules, generic competitors were not able to enter the market as the original product they referred to was no longer authorized on the market either. Thus, AstraZeneca did not only prevent parallel trade of the blockbuster drug but also delayed market entry of competitors in the above mentioned three markets (Csiszár 2012: 126). Preventing both parallel trade and generic competition, the European Commission analyzed the anticompetitive behavior of AstraZeneca in 2005. They found that AstraZeneca, being in a monopoly position because of its patent protection, was abusing its market dominant position to deter competition and violating Art. 102 TFEU. AstraZeneca was also found guilty for providing misleading information to patent protection officers when applying for supplementary protection certificates (SPC) with which they achieved extended patent protection (Csiszár 2012: 126). In 2010, however, the General Court of the EU, who reviewed the case again, ruled that no direct effect on parallel trade could be verified. Therefore, AstraZeneca violated Article 102 TFEU, delaying generic entry. In case of parallel imports, those violations did not apply, according to the findings of the General Court (2010[16]).

There has not been a similar case of this nature analyzed yet in the US. Since parallel trade is ruled more strictly in the US and not as commonly practiced as in the EU, performing alteration of administration forms might be more difficult in the US than in the EU.

Coming to a conclusion, it can be said, that deregistration of patent rights and more precisely providing differences in administration forms between different countries can prevent parallel trade without directly violating competition law. Still, this must not occur in context of generic entry, because the delay of generic entry through alteration

16 See General Court (2010), 'Judgment of the General Court in Case T-321/05', *Official Journal of the European Union C 221/33,* URL: http://goo.gl/tESsmn (retrieved May 10, 2016).

of administration forms violates Article 102 TFEU. Therefore, branded drug manufacturers can influence parallel trade competition by applying for patent protection for different admission forms in countries varying significantly in prices.

3.1.5 Dual Pricing

RPM, product change and arbitrage performed by producers are possibilities to not only prevent parallel trade, but also to deter generic entry. However, there exists another form of vertical restraints, allowing branded drug manufacturers to influence market entry of competitors, which is called "Dual Pricing". Dual pricing allows manufacturers to set different downstream prices in different market situations. In this special case, different prices for goods remaining on the market of origin and for goods being exported to other markets are charged. To examine it more closely, manufacturers will sell their drug at a low price to distributors under the condition that the distributor sells the drug only in the country of origin. If distributors want to sell the drug in another country, manufacturers will sell their drug to a higher price, equal to prices in the country of destination. Hence, distributors are not able to generate revenues as they have to pay the same price, they would pay in the importing country. (Matteucci and Reverberi 2016: 50). Matteucci and Reverberi (2016: 57), prove in that context that dual pricing can be treated equal to not allowing for parallel trade since the effects of both are the same. If dual pricing is enforceable, manufacturers keep investing in R&D to improve their drugs. They also serve the low price market, since they do not have to fear price competition in their high price markets. Governments of low price countries, tend to tolerate dual pricing as they benefit from it in the long run (Matteucci and Reverberi 2016: 57).

One of the most popular cases of such dual pricing is the case of GlaxoSmithKline Service unlimited (GSK) (former known as Glaxo Wellcome plc), a pharmaceutical originator drug producer. In 1998, GSK charged a higher downstream price for its drugs when distributors wanted to export the drug. When distributors assured GSK to sell the drugs in the domestic market, GKS only charged the usual prices. The prices for domestic sales were significantly lower as the prices for a parallel traded drugs, limiting the distributors' abilities to realize high mark ups when selling the drug in a high-price country (Stothers 2010: 123).

Analyzing the anticompetitive actions undertaken by GSK to prevent parallel trade, the European Commission decided in 2001, that GSK was not allowed to perform dual pricing as it violated Article 101(1) TFEU by restricting free trade (European

Commission 2001: 38[17]). In addition to that, GSK referred to Article 101(3) TFEU to plea for exception of violating Article 101(1) TFEU. They referred to increasing welfare through intensified R&D (Stothers 2010: 124). In that case, the European Commission dismissed GSK's request for exception, stating that welfare improvement did not coincide with the requirements of Article 101(3) TFEU to examine exceptions (European Commission 2001: 38[15]). After the decision of the European Commission, GSK appealed and the European Court of Justice reanalyzed the case. In 2009, the European Court of Justice analyzed the case of imposing different prices for different ways of distribution of GSK drugs. It also came to the decision that GSK was violating Article 101(1) TFEU and no exemptions from this regulation violation were applicable (European Court of Justice 2009[18]).

Again, I could not find a similar case in the US. However, as already shown, the EU and the US implement similar statuary provisions to prevent anticompetitive actions by originator drug manufacturers. Therefore, dual pricing would violate Sherman Act Section 1 by restricting free trade.

Dual pricing is an effective possibility to prevent parallel trade. Nevertheless, it violates Article 101(1) TFEU because of restricting competition and free trade. It reduces consumers' ability to access cheaper substitute products. Hence, it is only applicable if producers are able to prove that preventing parallel trade increases welfare to achieve a rule of reason approach. Furthermore, dual pricing relies on contracts between downstream and upstream firms that ensure punishment of producers if distributors cheat and sell their drugs in other countries without paying higher prices. Future research should therefore examine when dual pricing is attractive for originator manufacturers, with regard to contract cost.

3.2 Competitive Restraints under Reference Pricing

Parallel trade is a market situation that influences profits of originator drug manufacturers because of allowing for arbitrage and competition, even before patent termination. Above that, there exists another important aspect reducing originator manufacturers' profits already during market exclusivity times. As already addressed in chapter 2.4, regulatory provisions limit manufacturers' ability of free pricing and allow regulators to control pharmaceutical prices. When branded drug manufacturers are not

17 See European Commission (2001), '(2001/791/EC) Commission Decision of 8 May 2001', *Official Journal of the European Commission L 302/1-43*, URL: http://goo.gl/wQXd4b (retrieved May 11, 2016)

18 See European Court of Justice (2009), '(2009/C 282/02) Judgment of the Court (Third Chamber) of 6 October 2009', *Official Journal of the European Union C-282/2*, URL: http://goo.gl/EC8uvC (retrieved May 11, 2016).

able to generate monopoly profits while their products are patent protected, their incentive to innovate is reduced (Galizzi, Ghislandi, and Miraldo 2011: 18).

The most common regulation schemes practiced in the pharmaceutical industry are price cap regulation (PCR) and reference price regulation (RPR). Both schemes let regulators control the maximum prices at the retail level. The difference between both schemes is that RPR only sets a maximum reimbursement rate, where consumers have to pay additional cost out of pocket, leaving manufacturers the ability to charge higher prices. PCR, however, does not allow prices higher than the predefined reimbursement rate (Brekke, Holmas, and Straume 2011: 624). Recent studies analyze the different welfare effects under the use of PCR and RPR. They agree on the suggestion for regulators to use RPR as this leads to a more significant increase in competition and reduces drug prices more significantly than PCR (Brekke, Grasdal, and Holmas 2009: 183; Brekke, Holmas, and Straume 2011: 637). This conclusion is consistent with the observation of the international pharmaceutical markets, where a shift from PCR to RPR can be observed. With exception of the US pharmaceutical market, where none of both regulation schemes is applied, most EU countries, as well as the UK and Japan either changed their regulation form from PCR to RPR or directly implemented RPR (Vernon 2005: 1; Abbott and Vernon 2007: 293). Therefore, my intention is to only focus on RPR when presenting a possibility of originator producers to prevent competition.

The goal of RPR is to set prices for drugs below the monopoly price, a manufacturer would charge for the drug. The regulation is called "reference price regulation" because regulators set the reimbursed price equal to prices of similar drugs available on the market. In this case, other drugs serve as reference for the drug price. This reference can either include prices for the same drug or prices charged for similar drugs with same therapeutic effects. Accordingly, there are differences in computation of reference prices, leading to different regulation schemes in various countries (Galizzi, Ghislandi, and Miraldo 2011: 18). Regulators group drugs with similar therapeutic effects or similar active ingredients. As all drugs in this group treat similar illnesses, one price can be set for the whole group of products. When a new product applies for market admission, this group price serves as reference for determining reimbursement rates for the new drug (Bardey, Bommier, and Jullien 2010: 303).

The first form of RPR is the so-called "therapeutic reference pricing" (TRP). TRP groups all drugs that have the same therapeutic effect. Not only generics and their brand name drugs, but also similar drugs with different compounds are put into one group. Hence, TRP can be applied to new brand name drugs that apply for market approval (Galizzi, Ghislandi, and Miraldo 2011: 19). Another form of RPR is the so-called "generic reference pricing" (GRP). This form of RPR is used when patents for originator drugs have expired and generic competitors enter the market. Since generic competitor drugs are bioequivalent to the originator products, they can be put into one group and can be given the same reimbursement rate (Stargardt 2011: 4517). In their study, Leopold et al. (2012: 52) found that within the EU, TRP is used more often than GRP, with 23 of 27 member states applying TRP.

In addition to that, RPR also varies to the location of reference drugs. This differentiation of referenced drug prices is made between internal and external factors (Kaiser, et al. 2014: 174). The former clusters all similar products that are originated in the domestic market, focusing only on national market prices. External reference pricing considers only prices of equivalent drugs or forms of therapy from foreign markets. If external RPR is applied, only drugs of markets which are economically similar to the domestic market are considered. In both cases, a reimbursement rate is set either according to an average of all prices of the reference drugs or according to the minimum price available for one of the reference drugs (Leopold et al. 2012: 51).

As already explained above, empirical studies find, that RPR increases competition and decreases drug prices in the pharmaceutical sector. The reason why GRP regulation increases competition is examined by Ghislandi (2011: 1137). Ghislandi first affirms that, because generic drugs are cheaper substitutes for the originator drugs, manufacturers have an incentive to set prices for their drugs significantly low, serving as reference level for the GRP. In his study Ghislandi (2011) examines this statement and finds out, that competition does not directly take place at the reimbursement level, but rather at the level of distribution. According to Ghislandi (2011: 1139) GRP is a two stage game, where the reimbursement level R is set in the first stage, as a function of originator and generic drug prices p_{orig} and p_{gen} in the first period:

$$R(p_{orig}, p_{gen}) \,\forall \left\{R \in \mathbb{R} \parallel p_{gen} \leq R \leq p_{orig}\right\} \qquad (3.2)$$

Since generic drugs are direct substitutes, Bertrand competition can be assumed, forcing prices to equal marginal cost. However, in the second stage, which lasts all remaining periods, prices are set taking R as exogenously given. If the price for the branded drug is equal or smaller than the price for generic drugs, the originator drug will serve the whole market. Hence, generic manufacturers have an incentive to undercut originator drug prices. To prevent zero-profits due to Bertrand competition, generic manufacturers have an incentive to collude, setting a higher price than marginal cost and still serving as reference for the reimbursement level. Also there is a low incentive to cheat, because cheating would lead to all other firms performing grim trigger strategy in the following periods. In this case each firm generates zero profits. Nonetheless, Ghislandi (2011:

1139) claims that regulators would detect collusion of generic producers easily, as all generic producers setting prices above the level of R in the second stage would disclose collusive behavior. Thus, prices above marginal cost is not feasible. After a reimbursement price is set, the only possibility for manufactures to directly influence prices is at the level of distribution. This leads to competition for quantity through discounts for distributors (Ghislandi 2011: 1146).

TRP leads to prices of similar drugs being compared. Competition, therefore, also increases when TRP is applied as drugs within the same TRP group are imperfect substitutes (Kyle 2007: 91). This leads to reduction in drug prices according to Galizzi, Ghislandi, and Miraldo (2011: 25). In this context Lichtenberg and Philipson (2002: 663), were able to prove that the market entry of therapeutic equal competitor drugs reduced profits of originator manufacturers more significantly, than the introduction of generic entry. As I am going present ways to prevent competition arisen through generic market entry in the following chapters, this chapter focuses on possibilities to thwart competition that occurs while drugs are still patent protected. The focus of this chapter, therefore, lays on external reference pricing using TRP.

Like already explained above, external reference pricing groups all prices of similar medications (TRP) in an international context and determines the reimbursement rate as an average or minimum of all prices. This intends to converge prices in the referenced countries. (Leopold et al. 2012: 51). Since manufacturers are not able to directly influence the reimbursement rate set by the regulators, their intention is to find a way to circumvent significant reduction in reimbursement rates in high-price countries. Reference countries tend to be economically equal but consumers' willingness to pay can vary across those countries. Producers can therefore circumvent reduction in prices by not serving low price countries which are reference for high price countries. Those circumventions can be observed in international markets where some drugs are launched in one country but not in another, even if those countries are in similar economic situations (Kyle 2007: 88).

External reference pricing links countries' drug prices in a way that is comparable to the introduction of parallel trade. Hence, firms try to delay or even avoid market entry in those countries, that serve as reference for other countries (Danzon, Wang, and Wang 2005: 271). According to Kyle (2007: 91), originator manufacturers headquartered in countries with external reference pricing launch their products in less markets as this country negatively influences prices in other countries. In combination with parallel trade, a regulation that compares international prices negatively affects the launch of drugs in low price countries. As Danzon, Wang, and Wang (2005: 271) examine, originator manufacturers tend to launch their product only in high-price countries, not subjected to external price regulation, in order to hinder regulators to reduce the prices for their good. With this, they cannot only prevent reduction in reimbursed rates but also entry of parallel traded goods.

An example for this is Pfizer Inc.'s threat to not serve the French market in 2001. At the end of 1990s, Pfizer was under high pressure concerning price controls in France. Regulatory provisions reduced Pfizer's profits (Kyle 2007: 89). As a consequence, Pfizer signaled delayed market entry of their new innovations if French price controls would not be loosened (Gilbert and Rosenberg 2004).

Concerning the legal issues of not serving markets to circumvent price reduction occurring because of external TRP, it has to be said that there cannot be found direct violations against EU and US competition law. Both, the Sherman act, as well as EU-competition law articles focus on violation of competition rules if competition already exists or is directly deterred through anticompetitive behavior of companies (15 U.S.C §3; Article 101 TFEU). Patent protected originator drugs provide additional efficacy compared to other drugs that are already served on the market. While they are in some way one-of-a-kind, they do not face direct competition through perfect substitutes when being patent protected. Consequently, they are not deterring competition when refusing to enter the market. If this action is examined in a global context, however, not launching the pharmaceuticals in certain markets restrains parallel trade and affects competition and welfare. Prices remain higher in high price countries and consumers of not served countries have no access to innovations. Besides, not entering some markets has effects on consumers' health and therefore must be analyzed closely for violation of Article 102 TFEU. Furthermore, the EU in total is seen as one single market with free movement of goods. Refusing to serve one country restricts this free movement of goods stated in Article 101 TFEU. As the US is home country to most of the blockbuster innovating firms and the only country with almost no price control, it is not directly affected by the above mentioned actions and not discussed further concerning legal violations (Kyle 2007: 89).

Delaying entry in countries with low prices and strict price regulations can prevent parallel trade. If, additionally, low price countries are reference for high price countries' regulation schemes, not serving those countries helps originator manufacturers to circumvent competition and limit parallel trade. During my research I could not find hints concerning EU or US court of justices examining law violations as result of delayed entry. Hence this can be a loophole for manufactures to profitably prevent competition and should be examined further in future researches.

3.3 Restraints against Generic Entry

Both, parallel trade and regulatory provisions lead to competition for originator manufacturers, while their products are still patent protected. In addition to competition that already occurs during patent protection time, generic entry intensifies this competition after patents expired. As it is in branded drug manufacturers interest to generate monopoly profits as long as possible, deterring parallel trade and circumventing price reductions imposed by regulatory provision are not the only actions branded drug manufactures perform to deter competition. The following sub chapters will therefore present ways that producers use market exclusivity rights by using extended patent protections and intensifying brand loyalty of consumers.

3.3.1 Branded Generics

When patent protection has expired, generic competitors are allowed to enter the market, launching substitutes to the originator product. Similar to parallel traded drugs, generic drugs might not be observed as perfect substitutes to the brand name drug. Most consumers tend to see generic drugs as qualitatively different to the originator product, due to subjective aspects. For example, the fact that consumers already now the originator product and have to adjust to the new generic products impose switching costs for consumers. This is one reason, why originator drugs are able to compete with generic drugs, even if prices for generics are cheaper than the branded drug (Hudson 2000: 207). Therefore, it is in the manufacturers' interest to gain consumers' trust in their brand, so that consumers build loyalty to the originator drug. Brand loyal consumers rather tend to decline substitution of the drug they are loyal to. They are more willing to purchase the product than non-brand loyal consumers after the patent has expired and they have to bear the co-payment (the difference between retail price and reimbursement rate) (Costa-Font, Rudisill, and Tan 2014: 224). However, even if brand loyal consumers keep purchasing the originator drugs after patent expiry, this group of customers only amounts to some part of total demand that could be served by the manufacturer. In this context, Costa-Font, McGuire, and Varol (2014: 1) affirm that after patent expiration, market shares of originator manufacturers decrease by about 50%, even if there are brand loyal consumers purchasing the drug. Manufacturers, therefore, are interested in finding ways to generate high market shares after their patent has expired.

The time between patent termination and generic entry can vary, and often there is no direct shift from monopoly to competition. There rather exists a time lag between patent termination and generic entry. This is because generic producers have to prove the therapeutic efficacy, safeness, and active ingredients of their drug to be similar to the branded drug. The proof of bioequivalence can take up to three to five years. (Costa-

Font, McGuire, and Varol 2014: 2). To reduce the lag between patent termination and generic entry, US and EU law allow generic companies to research, produce, and advertise their generic before patent termination (98th United States Congress 1984[19]; European Union 2004: 35[20]). In the US, this is also known under the term "Hatch-Waxman-Act". It grants the first generic producer to apply for market approval 180 days of exclusivity in advertising and marketing before any other generic drug can enter the market. It also allows generic producers to use clinical trial data of the branded drug, in order to save cost and time of additional clinical trials. This sets an incentive for generic firms to enter the market as early as possible. On the other hand, the Hatch-Waxman-Act tries to set additional incentives for originator manufacturers to keep investing in R&D. Originator manufacturers are granted data exclusivity for specified time after their market entry (Stotland Weiswasser and Danzis 2004: 591, 603).

Manufacturers, moreover, can answer market entry of competitors by launching a so-called "branded generic". When analyzing this action of originator manufacturers, closer attention has to be paid to literature, when referring to the term "branded generics". Two different definitions of the term can be found when reviewing literature. One part of literature refers to "branded generics" (or "authorized generics") as produced and launched by generic companies. Branded generics launched by generic producers offer the same therapeutic effect as the originator drug but through some alteration in active ingredients are not bioequivalent and can receive a patent for this alteration. Therefore, they are sold under a brand name and not the active ingredient's name (Danzon and Furukawa 2008: 226). In the second case an originator manufacturer launches the branded drug under a generic name for a cheaper price than before patent termination. To do so, the firm can either produce and sell the drug or sell licenses for the drug to generic companies in exchange for royalties (Hollis 2002: 725). In this case, literature also often refers to those drugs as „pseudo-generics“ (Hollis 2005: 329). In the following I refer to the latter one as „branded generics".

As generic competitors are able to advertise their product prior to market entry, brand name manufacturers are able to observe entry strategies of their competitors. In addition to that, brand name manufacturers are able to sell their generic version before competitors are able to enter, because they are the owners of the patent rights and do not have to wait for patent termination (Hollis 2005: 329; Reiffen and Ward 2007: 254). Hence, they can induce competition for generic producers and discourage other possible

19 See 98th United States Congress (1984) 'Drug Price Competition and Patent Term Restoration Act of 1984', *98 STAT. 1585 Public Law 98-417*, URL: https://goo.gl/LXbXlo (retrieved May 10, 2016).

20 See footnote 3.

producers from entering the market, as originator firms are able to already secure market shares (Berndt, et al. 2007: 790).

Even as Hollis (2005: 330) suspects positive welfare effects for consumers in the short run, because they are able to access a cheaper version of their medicine before the expected market entry of generics, Hollis also expects negative impact of pseudo-generic entry in the long run. In consensus with this, Reiffen and Ward (2007: 263) are able to prove that prices in the case of pseudo generic entry are higher in the long run than without the incumbent producing a generic product. In the case of launching pseudo-generics, the originator manufacturer would be price leader. Kong and Seldon (2004: 83) prove that branded generics reduce the amount of generic companies entering the market as entrants are deterred when originator manufacturers are already in possession of generic market shares (Reiffen and Ward 2007: 263). In this context, Garnier and Trinquard (2010: 301) show that it is always profitable for originators to launch authorized generics. They state that the decision to produce pseudo generics can be seen as a form of a Stackelberg game, where the originator firm is Stackelberg leader. Garnier and Trinquard (2010: 301) assume that there are not many additional costs for originator companies to produce branded generics as originator firms are already producing the drug. If originators do not launch a pseudo generic, their profit will be the market share they realize with only supplying a branded product s_b times the price for the branded product p_b, under the assumption that marginal costs equal zero. The first generic manufacturer then generates profits of the total generic market share s_g times the price for the generic product p_g less the set up cost for market entry F.

$$\pi_b^{NPG} = s_b p_b \tag{3.3}$$

$$\pi_g^{NPG} = s_g p_g - F \tag{3.4}$$

Garnier and Trinquard (2010: 299) assume further, that consumers' utility differs when using the generic drug, as they observe originator drugs offering higher quality and therefore receive discounted utility U_g when getting the generic drug version. The utility is discounted by factor φ, as this factor describes the type of customer on an interval [0,1].

$$U_b = u - p_b \tag{3.5}$$

$$U_g = \varphi u - p_g \tag{3.6}$$

As Garnier and Trinquard (2010: 299) use a Stackelberg-competition game, backwards induction leads to the solution of the originator firm realizing profits of

$$\pi_b^{NPG} = \frac{u}{2} \tag{3.7}$$

and the generic manufacturer of realizing profits of [21]

$$\pi_g^{NPG} = \frac{u}{4} - F \tag{3.8}$$

If, however, the originator manufacturer launches a pseudo generic, the manufacturer is able to generate the above shown branded firm's profit in addition to half of the generics' profit as the originator is able to secure half of the generics market share.

$$\pi_b^{PS} = s_b p_b + \frac{1}{2} s_g p_g \tag{3.9}$$

$$\pi_g^{PG} = \frac{1}{2} s_g p_g - F \tag{3.10}$$

Solving this game through backwards induction, originator manufacturers realize even higher shares than without launching pseudo generics.

$$\pi_b^{PG} = \frac{5}{8} u \tag{3.11}$$

$$\pi_g^{PG} = \frac{1}{8} u - F \tag{3.12}$$

Hence, Garnier and Trinquard (2010: 301) show that pseudo generics can effectively deter generics' market entry, if set up costs F are sufficiently high, as entry would not be profitable as long as

$$F > \frac{1}{8} u \tag{3.13}$$

The possibility of producing own generics has found large attention by brand name manufacturers in the last two centuries. Most of the companies performing the launch of branded generics were large pharmaceutical companies such as Ely Lilly, Merck and GSK (Reiffen and Ward 2007: 252; Kong and Seldon 2004: 73). One of the most popular companies to market branded generic drugs is GSK. In 2003, GSK expected generics to enter the market after patent protection for their depression drug Paxil (paroxetine) expired. In order to prevent significant losses in sales, GSK produced a generic substitute to Paxil and sold it through the pharmaceutical distributor Par Pharmaceutical (GlaxoSmithKline 2003). With this production of a branded generic, GSK was able to enter the market before other generic manufacturers entered and secured valuable market shares and profits (Hollis 2005: 332). Similar actions were undertaken by Bristol Meyers Squib, where it sold authorized generics for the Diabetes drug Glucophage XR to Par Pharmaceutical in exchange for Royalties (Abboud 2004).

21 Note: As this profit is dependent on the indifferent customer φ is omitted in the final profit functions.

Being the first generic entrant to the market includes high expenses on entry, as patents have to be challenged by the first entrant prior to patent termination. However, this cost is smoothed as first generic entrants can capture high market shares because of being the only cheaper version of the originator drug. If, on the other hand, brand name manufacturers launch pseudo-generics, this profits will decrease for the first entrant, as consumers tend to avoid switching costs. This decreases generic producers' incentive to enter markets when knowing that there will be an authorized generic (Hollis 2005: 333). From a legal point of view, it can be said that pseudo-generics do not violate statutory provisions of the Sherman Act and EU competition law. Introducing direct competition to the branded product, originator manufactures do not act in an anticompetitive way that threatens competition but rather introduce competition early. Even as generic manufacturers tried to accuse brand manufacturers who launched pseudo-generics for interfering competition and violating the Hatch-Waxman-Act lawsuits were thrown out by the FDA (Hollis 2005: 332). Generic manufacturers argue that the Hatch-Waxman Act was imposed to promote generic competition and grant consumers early access to cheaper versions of the originator product. The launch of pseudo-generics, on the other hand, cannibalizes the secured 180 days exclusive market rights of generics and reduce generic manufacturers profits and incentive to enter (Reiffen and Ward 2007: 255). Consequently, fewer generic competitors are likely to enter the market which in return reduces competition.

On the other hand, Berndt et al. (2007: 798) as well as Kong and Seldon (2004: 83) conclude that, even if generic entry is delayed by pseudo-generics, significant price increases for generics cannot be found. This is contradictory to the findings of Reiffen and Ward (2007: 263) and hence should be analyzed again more closely. All three, nonetheless, agree on increasing market shares of originator manufacturers and the ability for them to generate higher profits than without the launch of pseudo generics.

Coming to a conclusion, it can be said that launching branded generics is a possibility for branded drug producers to secure market shares when facing generic competition and influence the degree of generic entry without violating competition law. Since EU law does not offer exclusivity rights for generic manufactures like the US Hatch-Waxman Act, it is even easier for originator manufacturers in the EU to launch pseudo-generics without violating the law. This creates an incentive for manufacturers to invest in R&D, as they are at least partly able to circumvent losses of market shares and profit. However, anticompetitive behavior should be further analyzed by authorities concerning the launch of pseudo-generics, as it allows manufacturers to keep high market shares and a dominant market position with which they can influence prices and influence welfare negatively.

3.1.4 Product Hopping

Producing own generic products is one way for pharmaceutical manufacturers to delay or even deter entry of generic competition without facing charges for violating competition and antitrust law. Nevertheless, there exist further possibilities for brand name manufacturers to prevent competition through generic market entry by using patent extensions. As manufacturers find therapy improvements for their products, during time of marketing, they can change their product to be better adjusted to side-effects. Patent rights secure originator manufacturer's monopoly power and grant them exclusive market rights. If new patents for the same branded drugs are filed, this is called product Evergreening or Patent-Life-Cycle Management (Bansal, et al 2009: 299). There are two different ways of drug Evergreening. I present the first way in this chapter and the second in the following chapter.

The first way of Evergreening is changing the drug to produce an incremental improvement of the drug. Producers then set incentives for consumers to purchase the new version of the drug. This form of changing drugs to achieve patent extension can be found in literature under the name "Product Hopping" (Chen 2008: 1427). Product hopping is an important way to secure extended exclusivity rights as it grants producers SPCs. These secondary patents grant producers additional exclusivity rights for the same product (Csiszár 2012: 126). As already stated above generic manufacturers can challenge patents when finding gaps in the patents of originator manufacturers. Especially the Hatch-Waxman Act in the US sets an incentive for generic manufactures to do so because of the exclusive marketing period when first entering the market, prior to patent expiration. However, originator manufacturers are allowed to improve their drugs and file additional patents for those improvements, taking away generic manufacturers' ability to challenge patents and enter early (Hemphill and Sampat 2012: 328-329).

In the case of product hopping originator manufacturers produce the same drug they own patent rights for and change one component of the active ingredient to achieve an alteration of the already existing drug. With the same therapeutic efficacy and patent protection they produce a me-too drug (Gilbert 2015: 39). As both, in the US and the EU, new products are granted exclusivity rights, this delays generic entry. Even if generic competitors are allowed to file challenges, they are not allowed to do so at point of market entry of the new drug. In the US, generic companies are allowed to file challenges earliest five years after market approval of the patented drug. In the EU generic companies even need to wait eight to ten years after approval. This is secured through the data exclusivity rights explained in chapter 2.2 (Grabowski and Moe 2008: 87-88). Hence, branded drug producers can launch their advanced drug version when they observe market applications of generic competitors. After the change of ingredients, the manufacturer engages in significant advertising of the new product version. Goal of this promotion is to incite physicians to prescribe the advanced product version and therefore generate a shift in demand from the old product to the new one. Generic competitors who now enter the market, are only able to offer bioequivalent drugs to the old version of the branded drug (Wittkowsky 2001: 141). As originator producers promote the new product version to consumers and physicians, consumers are more likely to choose the latest product version. Consequently, pharmacists are not able to substitute the drug through a generic version anymore, as generic competitors only possess market approval for bioequivalent versions of the old drug version. Thus, market shares for generic competitors are reduced (Gilbert 2015: 40). Following this hop of product features, generic competitors have to also change the ingredients of their product to be able to compete for market shares with the new version of originator drugs. Because this means production changes and new proof of bioequivalence for the generic manufacturers, a delay in market entry of generic drugs is certain (Silber and Kuritz 2010: 121).

Furthermore, generic manufacturers might also need to file additional patent litigations for additional product versions in order to be granted market access. Originator manufacturers can respond to this litigation by filing patent infringement litigations. As a consequence of generic manufacturers infringing patents, originator manufacturers are granted additional 30-month exclusive market rights in the US where generic market entry is restrained (21. U.S.C. §355 (j) (5) (B) (iii)). However, the delay of generic entry only works sufficiently, if originator producers are able to shift total demand for their drug from the old product version to the new one.

Product hopping under legal aspects, yet, has to be examined more closely, as in history it led to different outcomes (Gilbert 2015: 40). To understand the different approaches of courts analyzing pharmaceutical product hopping, one has to know that there are differences in the extent of hopping. The first form of product hopping is the so-called “soft” switch of product forms. In this case, the manufacturer launches a me-too drug as additional alternative to the already existing drug. This leaves consumers and physicians more alternatives to choose from, when deciding which treatment to take. The second form of product hopping is the so-called “hard” version of switching from one product to the other. In this case, consumers are prevented from purchasing the old version of

the drug, because it is supplied under strict, limited terms only or withdrawn from the market in total. (Ginsburg, Wong-Ervin, and Wright 2015: 2). Both forms of product hopping have been applied by originator producers as will be shown in the following.
In 2001 AstraZeneca's heartburn and ulcer drug Prilosec (omeprazole) faced patent termination. Before patent protection expired, Prilosec was the blockbuster drug of AstraZeneca allowing them to generate significant profits. With the termination of their patent, AstraZeneca observed competition threats through generic entry. To thwart this competition, AstraZeneca changed the active substance of Prilosec from omeprazole to esomeprazole and named the new version "Nexium". After the launch of Nexium, AstraZeneca stopped advertising Prilosec and started to only promote Nexium. As a consequence, demand for Prilosec decreased and Nexium demand increased significantly (Silber and Kuritz 2010: 123; Chen 2008: 1490). Competitors who entered the market with generic substitutes for Prilosec could only sell their products when the older version of AstraZeneca's drug Prilosec was described by physicians. If physicians, albeit, prescribed Nexium, pharmacists were not allowed to substitute the drug.
Subsequently, generic companies and purchasers proceeded against AstraZeneca's product hopping, in 2006, calling it to be unlawful as it limited free trade. Competitors also sued AstraZeneca for creating a monopoly, unlawfully using their market power and therefore violating antitrust laws (Silber and Kuritz 2010: 124). The court, however, found that introducing Nexium to the market offered additional benefit to consumers because more alternatives were available (Chen 2008: 1497). Silber and Kuritz (2010: 122), moreover, explain that district courts dismissed the lawsuit against AstraZeneca by referring to another case, where the Supreme Court ruled that offering innovations to consumers is per se legal (United States Supreme Court 1980[22]). This also was the most important argument as AstraZeneca did not restrict consumers' alternative treatments but enriched the market with a different alternative. Consumers were not forced to change their demand. Competitors were not actively prevented from market entry, as they were able to either offer a generic version of the old drug, or perform a product hop on their own (Gilbert 2015, 42). The district court, in addition, argued that originator manufacturers do not violate competition law when offering a me-too product, while simultaneously offering the older version of the product, even if it decreases generic manufacturers abilities to free-ride innovation processes (Ginsburg, Wong-Ervin, and Wright 2015: 3).

22 See United States Supreme Court (1980), 'Berkey Photo Inc. v. Eastman Kodak Co. 444 U.S. 1095 (1980)', *On Petitions for Writs of Certiorari to the United States Court of Appeals for the Second Circuit*, URL: https://goo.gl/P5tWGk (retrieved May 10, 2016).

In contrast to the AstraZeneca case, which was ruled to be a legal action, there were other cases where the district courts found originator companies guilty for persuading infringement of competition law. One of these cases is the case of Abbott Labs and Fournier producing TriCor (fenofibrate), a Cholesterol-lowering drug. Abbot and Fournier (from now on only referred to as Abbott) received patent protection for TriCor in the 1990s. At the beginning of the 2000s, the generic manufacturer Teva Pharmaceuticals Inc. (Teva) applied for market approval of their generic TriCor version. As Abbott faced threat of generic entry, they participated in product hopping to thwart entry of Teva's generic drug (Gilbert 2007: 69). Abbott changed the administration form of TriCor from capsules to tablets in order to create a new product for which Teva did not own generic approval. However, Abbott did not only promote the advanced drug but also withdrew the market approval for the old drug formula, leaving consumers no choice but to purchase the later version. This is why Teva had no reference drug anymore as the company wanted to apply market approval for capsules. After Teva adjusted their generic drug to the new version of TriCor, Abbott amended their product again. Abbott also removed the older version of their product from the market (Silber and Kuritz 2010: 122). Thus, Teva had to invest in changing their drug again to be able to enter the market. Consequently, Teva stopped investing in amendments and applied for patent protection for their own brand name drug "Lofibra", offering a me-too product (Chen, 2008: 1493).

After entering the market with their own brand name drug, Teva proceeded against Abbot because of abusing monopoly position to thwart competition. The difference to the case of AstraZeneca was that Abbott sufficiently shifted 100% of demand from the old drug version to the new drug version because of withdrawing the old drug from the market. Plaintiffs therefore argued that Abbott denied consumers choices of different alternatives. Consumers would, hence, not benefit from the introduction of the latest TriCor version, as foreclosure of competitors coerced consumers to buy the new drug (Chen 2008: 1494; Silber and Kuritz 2010: 123). In the Abbott case, the US district court decided that a violation of antitrust law was existing. Abbot was found guilty of forcing consumers to purchase the new version of the drug. Simultaneously, generic manufacturers were not able to successfully enter the market, as the reference drug was withdrawn from the market.

The two cases analyzed above suggest that product hopping has pro-competitive effects if the manufacturing firm does not coerce consumers to switch demand to their advanced drug version by removing the old version from the market. If, however, coercion of consumers occurs and generic competitors are not able to enter the market, this is an abuse of monopoly power that harms consumers. Consequently, US antitrust and EU competition laws are violated as they prohibit abuse of market dominant position that restricts free trade and harms consumers (15 U.S.C §1-§2; Article 102 TFEU). Furthermore, European generic manufacturers claim that new versions of drugs do not offer additional benefits to consumers as they are insignificantly changing effects of former drugs (Parker and Mooney 2007: 236). As a result, product hopping cannot be stated to be per se legal but rather has to be analyzed according to the rule of reason approach as different types of product hopping affect consumers in different ways (Silber and Kuritz 2010: 122).

Even, if the (anti-)competitive effects of product hopping depend on the differences in switches originator producers perform, benefit for consumers cannot be taken directly into account when examining those effects. First, consumers are not able to directly influence their demand, as the physician prescribing the drug determine which drug to take. Second, Gilbert (2015: 40), and Ginsburg, Wong-Ervin, and Wright (2015: 3) argue that even coercion of consumers to switch demand can increase their benefit. They argue, that consumers are often dull in adoption of new drugs. If, through coercion, this dullness is overcome, manufacturers have a higher incentive to invest in innovations as they can be certain that their product will be adapted (Gilbert 2015: 40). In addition to that, Ginsburg, Wong-Ervin, and Wright (2015: 3) propose that consumers also benefit from slight changes in drugs, even if they are observed as negligible for market participants other than the patient, since they might improve quality of living for patients.

Product hopping is a chance for manufacturers to secure market shares and to be able to generate higher profits when facing generic competition. However, originator manufacturers cannot withdraw their old products from the market as this violates competition law. From a regulator's perspective, though, product hopping should be analyzed more closely in future studies because it does not only offer benefits for consumers when "soft switches" are performed but can also raise healthcare expenditures.

3.1.5 Extending Indication Approval

Product hopping, as one part of patent Evergreening, can be a successful tool to delay the entry of generic drugs. Nevertheless, as it can lead to violation of antitrust laws, originator producers found Extending Indication Approval to be another way to evergreen their patents and achieve extend market exclusivity, which I present in the following.

Patents grant originator manufacturers the right for exclusively promoting and supplying their product for a specified amount of years. Nonetheless, even during the time of patent protection, other producers are able to challenge patents and cause the IPR holder to lose exclusivity rights (Harrhoff and Reitzig 2004: 444). When applying for patent protection, manufacturers have to specify the breadth of their patent, meaning the therapeutic effect and the ambit they want the patent to cover. Hence, there are differences in patent applications and the breadth of ambits and therapeutic effects they are applied for. Patents can either only protect compounds and indications or can cover the whole breadth of a drug (Grabowski and Moe 2008: 87). According to Harrhoff and Reitzig (2004: 458), patent protection causes asymmetric information between the patentee and the competitor. This is because the patent office remarks parts of the patent which are challengeable by competitors due to not offering significant innovations to already existing formulations. Originators, thus, have advances in knowledge about challengeable loopholes in their patent. Moreover, according to Reitzig (2004: 940), the patent breadth asset value defines a patents value. Lanjouw and Schankermann (2001: 131) also state that the higher the patent value, the more competitors are attracted to the markets and the more likely those competitors will challenge the patents. Harrhoff and Reitzig (2004: 463, 475) confirm this proposition, adding that patentees owning high-value patents can achieve settlements with competitors more easily, because they are able to offer licensing contracts for branded generics, due to the breadth of the patent. Consequently, patents with a great size of patent family attract more challengers but are stronger to oppose the attacks. Patents with a small breadth, however, are less likely to face challenge but are weaker to be defended (Harrhoff and Reitzig 2004: 458). Originator producers, therefore, have to decide between filing a small patent, less attracting challenges or a large patent, being more robust against challenges.

During the years of drug life-cycle-management, branded drug manufacturers often find their drugs to treat additional diseases to the one they were created for. For example, during clinical trials manufacturers have to prove that their drug does not harm patients' lives and they also have to test for side effects. Those tests help manufacturers to not only outline negative side-effects, but may also show therapeutic effectiveness for other diseases (Grabowski and Moe 2008: 85). In this case, it can be profitable for the manufacturer to file patent protection not only for the treatment of the disease the drug was created for but also for treating another disease. This is the origin of the second Evergreening approach to delay generic entry by adding indications. In the following, I refer to this as "Extending Indication Approval" or "strategic patenting", as Blind, Cremers, and Mueller (2009: 428) define it in their paper.

An example for strategic patenting was made by Pfizer who originally invented Viagra (sildenafil) for treating hypertension but later filed patent application for treatment of erectile dysfunction (Dwivedi, Hallihosur, and Rangan 2010: 327). Following this procedure, patents can be applied not only for one treatment of diseases but for various diseases, if the manufacturer can prove the therapeutic efficiency for the disease.

Nevertheless, as Lanjouw and Schankermann (2001: 131) examine, the wider the patent protection, the higher the incentive for generic competitors to try patent infringement. Manufacturers, knowing treatment effects for several diseases, are not obliged to file patent protection for all ambits, their drug treats. Knowing that their application for more than one treatment attracts generic competitors to challenge the patent leads originators to keep the value of the patent as low as possible. For that reason, they are filing patents only for one treatment, waiting for the patent to expire and then file for a new treatment (Dwivedi, Hallihosur, and Rangan 2010: 326). The extension of indication approval allows manufacturers to keep filing multiple patents for the same drug and expand the years of patent protection. In the US, for example, additional indication for a drug grants originator manufacturers three extra years of data exclusivity after approval of the new indication (Huskamp et al. 2008: 605).

Strategic Patenting does not only help originator manufacturers to reduce the patent value of their drug and generic competitors' incentives to challenge it, it also helps them to expand exclusivity rights for the brand name drug. Generics have an incentive to challenge patent protection to enter early and therefore having a first mover advantage, as they are able to secure large market shares being the only cheaper drug version available (Bohari, Mariuzzo, and Polanski, 2015: 2). If, however, no challenge is filed, generics are not allowed to enter until all patents for the drug have expired. In this case, originator manufacturers are able to apply for patent protection for the treatment of another disease and expand the time of patent protection by up to 20 additional years (Hemphill and Sampat 2012: 328). Even if challenges are submitted, originators can file infringement to achieve 30 months stay, as explained in chapter 3.3.1 and then apply for market approval for another treatment, granting them further three years of exclusivity (Goldman et al. 2011: 84). Hence, generic competition can be delayed as generic manufacturers' ability to access clinical trial data, they need to prove bioequivalence for, is delayed by three years. This allows the manufacturer to still be able to realize high prices for their brand name drug and secure market shares over an extended period of time. Nonetheless, generic competitors are able to enter the market with a generic substitute for the therapeutic treatment which has lost patent protection. (Parker and Mooney 2007: 239).

The extension of exclusivity, nevertheless, bears some risks for the manufacturer. As other companies can detect additional treatment of the drug they can either file patent protection on their own, for the second indication or, if the indication is approved but not patent protected, generic companies might enter the market with generic substitutes for the not patent protected indication. An example for this is GSK's Parkinson's Disease (PD) drug Requip (ropinirol), which was also approved for treating Restless Legs Syndrome (RLS). Generic producers were able to enter the market with ropinirol drugs for treating RLS, as Requip had market approval for both indications but had no patent protection for treating RLS. This is why competitors were not infringing patent rights and only had to prove bioequivalence without performing any clinical trials. They just labeled their generic drugs to treating RLS and not PD, performing so-called "skinny labelling" (Wittkowsky 2001: 141). If, however, additional indications are not approved, it requires competitor manufacturers to perform clinical trials proving the effectiveness and safety of their own product version. This imposed extra cost of R&D which generic companies try to avoid by freeriding on the clinical trials of originator companies (Grabowski and Moe 2008: 86). Also, originator manufacturers have to bear cost of R&D for additional patent applications, as they have to prove the safeness and efficiency of their drug. Notwithstanding, as they already performed clinical trials, they can use results from those trials and save expenses that other producers would have to pay (Grabowski and Moe 2008: 85).

Originator manufacturers face cost of new patent filing for different indications. The question is, therefore, whether it is profitable for brand name manufacturers to perform strategic patenting. Regarding actions taken by originator companies in the last two decades, Evergreening and especially extending indication approval is an often used mechanism to delay generic entry[23]. Hence, it needs to be analyzed, when it is profitable for originator manufacturers to perform extending indication approval. The total cost of originator products consists of expenditures for R&D including clinical trials, patent application and post launch R&D processes, as well as post-launch promotion and production cost. As already explained in chapter 2.2, R&D cost amount to the greatest share of total cost and are more or less fixed. Production cost, on the other hand, are variable and very low compared to the cost of development. Thus, marginal cost for production are converging to zero, leading to companies realizing profits as long as additional output is produced (Huskamp et al. 2008: 605). If producers already know

[23] Merck used it to extend protection for Prosar, its prostate enlargement drug, by seeking patent protection for the indication of male pattern baldness. Eli Lilly extended protection by filing patent for Atomoxetine not only for depression but also for attention deficit hyperactivity disorder, as two of many other companies (Gupta et al. 2010: 4).

further indications for their drug and possess market approval for it, they are able to save most of the R&D expenditures and launch the drug for low extra marginal cost. According to Huskamp et al. (2008: 605) it is therefore always profitable to extend exclusivity to be able to generate higher profits, when facing only small R&D and almost no marginal cost. However, if further indications need to be found during another R&D process, the originator company must weigh the additional cost against the benefit. As Grabowski and Moe (2008: 85) affirm, in their paper about innovation of new cancer therapies, the search for other indications can amount to another $100 million, as other indications can impose the need of additional clinical trials. In this case the originator producer must calculate profits from exclusivity extension and see if it is profitable to invest in extension. Nevertheless, concerning blockbuster drugs, this investment can still be profitable, as reduction in profits through generic entry can likely exceed $100 million (Grabowski and Moe 2008: 85). When Eli Lilly's anti-depression drug Prozac (fluoxetine), for example, experienced generic competition their revenues decreased by 66% from $ 2.7 billion to $1.79 billion, which approximates revenue losses of $ 920 million. In that case investing in exclusivity extensions could have been profitable (Simons 2004). This profitability was shown by GSK, filing additional approval for its anti-depression drug Paxil (paroxetine) to be an indication for generalized anxiety disorder, before the patent protection for the original indication expired (Huskamp et al. 2008: 604).

Nonetheless, even if strategic patenting promises further profits for originator manufacturers, its primary goal is to prevent generic competitors from entering the market. Therefore, questions concerning its legal justifications arise (Blind, Cremers, and Mueller 2009: 429; Parker and Mooney 2007: 239). As strategic patenting is part of the Evergreening process, similar legal aspects that apply for product hopping also apply for strategic patenting. Different to the case of product hopping, yet, the length of patent protection can vary for additional indications. If indications are found for rare diseases, extension can take up to seven years (Grabowski and Moe 2008: 89). Since complementary approval of indication concerns treatments of other diseases, producers cannot perform a "switch" in demand. Thus, it can be argued that patients are not coerced to purchase the originator drug. No violation of antitrust law applies as it was ruled that invention of additional drugs is legal per se (Ginsburg, Wong-Ervin, and Wright 2015: 3). Besides, patients suffering from another disease can benefit from the complementary patent applications since there are further treatments available. Concerning violation of Article 101-103 TFEU and the Sherman Act, I could not find a case where strategic patenting, the way I defined it above, was not permissible. This might be the case, as producers do not directly abuse monopoly power and consumers are not harmed but rather benefit from new drugs because additional drug alternatives are offered. Furthermore, patients with rare diseases can benefit. Originator manufacturers are usually reserved to provide drugs for rare diseases as they tend to serve relatively small demand and therefore seem less profitable[24]. If, on the other hand, the manufacturer finds the drug to also treat one of those diseases, the producer is more likely to offer the drug for treatment of the rare disease since cost for additional approval are significantly lower (Goldman et al. 2011: 85). In future research, nevertheless, it should be examined more closely if Article 102 TFEU and Sherman Act Section 2 (15 U.S.C § 2) are violated, as free trade of pharmaceuticals is restricted due to delayed generic entry and delay of consumers' abilities to obtain cheaper versions of the drugs.

It was shown in this chapter, that there are several actions branded drug manufacturers can perform to restrict competition. However, it must be said that the actions preventing competition in total often violate antitrust and competition law in the US and EU and are not always applicable without facing charges. Concerning the delay of competition, on the other hand, there are several actions that do not violate statutory provisions and therefore are feasible by producers. Finally, a mixture of some of the above mentioned actions can be profitable to delay generic entry. Even if this means higher prices for consumers, regulators should consider not to intervene those actions, as they can set an incentive for manufacturers to further invest in R&D. In the long-run, this can benefit consumers due to enhanced medication and therapy standards.

24 These drugs are so-called „Orphan-Drugs“

4. Interactions Between Two or More Firms

All of the strategies presented in chapter 3 presented actions of originator companies to stave off generic and parallel trade competition were performed only by the originator producer. In all these cases no competitor actively participated in deterrence of competition and restricting consumers' access to alternative products. Even if deterring competition is imposed for the originator manufacturer to realize higher prices and profits, cooperation between competitors can also lead to extended exclusivity rights of the branded drug manufacturer. These collaborations often occur based on some of the above mentioned actions to thwart competition and are used to intensify anticompetitive effects. Therefore, this chapter will present actions to deter competition involving more than one pharmaceutical company as intensification of before performed anticompetitive actions by branded manufacturers only.

4.1 Pay for Delay

After losing market exclusivity rights, a brand manufacturer is likely to also face considerable losses in sales of the patent protected drug (Simons 2014). In chapter 3.3 I presented the possibility to deter competition by extending patent protection through changing the product or indication. These changes and applications of new patents for the same drug component can be challenged by generic manufacturers. Following Hemphill and Sampat (2012: 328) the challenges tend to be rather successful as complementary patents, issued at a later point of time, are more vulnerable to challenges and infringements. Hence, brand manufactures need to secure the exclusivity of their new patents, otherwise additional patent applications will be useless.

In this case, a successful action to deter competition and challenges for additional patents can involve one or more companies to find an agreement on time of entry of generic products. This agreement consists of some kind of collusion between the participating companies to reach a settlement (Kimbrough and Sheremeta 2013: 285). The settlement is often referred to as „pay for delay", "reverse settlement" or „reverse payment settlement" (Carrier 2014: 7; Peritz 2013: 160; Chen 2008; 1483). In most cases the pay for delay arrangement is implemented in combination with product hopping. It does not only delay generic entry but also secures the approval and market exclusivity of the new patent as no challenge litigations occur. Especially later filed patents tend to be prone to challenges and therefore may need further protection (Hemphill and Sampat 2012: 328). Moreover, manufacturers can shift the demand from the old drug to the latest drug version without already competing for demand through generic substitutes. When demand is already shifted, brand manufacturers do not have to fear generic entry anymore (Carrier 2014: 8).

As the name of the settlement already indicates, the agreement involves some kind of payment from the originator manufacturer to the generic competitor to delay generic market entry (Schildkraut 2004: 1033). Following Carrier (2010: 1015) this agreement between the two parties can be regarded as an allocation of time that divides the market, similar to an allocation of territory. The originator company gains the territory for a certain amount of time. Even as the term „payment“ implies the transaction of money between the two settling parties, reverse payment settlements do not necessarily involve money transactions but can also involve transactions of non-monetary goods. An example for the non-monetary transactions are authorized generics. According to the Federal Trade Commission (FTC), in almost 50% of reverse settlement cases, not selling authorized generics are involved as non-monetary payment (FTC Bureau of Competition 2013). If branded generics are launched, generic companies lose significant market shares and profits during their period of exclusivity[25]. Thus, originator manufacturers can agree on not selling authorized generics or selling licenses for the production of a branded generic to the generic competitor in return for the generic producer to delay market entry (Carrier 2014: 9). If a second generic firm challenges the patent, the branded drug manufacturer can again threat to launch an authorized generic through the first generic producer who agreed to the settlement. If the second challenger does not agree on settlement, the originator can launch an authorized generic and can compensate profit losses through royalties the first generic has to pay. In this case, the originator company only has to weigh the revenue losses from offering a branded generic to the revenues the originator gains through license fees. Moreover, through the reverse payment the generic drug producer keeps the first mover advantage while the originator can still generate monopoly profits (Bohari, Mariuzzo, and Polanski 2015: 4-5). In addition to that, Carrier (2014: 7) states, that the size of the payments can signal market dominance of originator manufacturers if they are able to secure weak patents with this payment. The higher the payment, the higher is the patent’s value and the more an originator manufacturer can lose through competition. Hence, branded drug manufacturers have a higher willingness to pay to delay entry and generate monopoly profits. Furthermore, the first generic entrant usually gains large market shares. (Bohari, Mariuzzo, and Polanski 2015: 5).

25 Here: the 180-day exclusivity of generic marketing granted by the Hatch-Waxman Act, where the first-filler generic is the only generic on the market.

Since an agreement between the two parties leads to an extrajudicial settlement, some courts are inhibited to rule against pay for delay settlements as both, time (opportunity) cost and cost for litigations are saved (Chen 2008: 1483). Nonetheless, reverse payment settlements find significant attention in the literature concerning scrutiny of violation of antitrust law. For pharmaceutical manufacturers, a pay for delay action can be rather profitable as loopholes in antitrust law allow for those actions to not be per se illegal (Peritz 2013: 166). Even though the branded drug producer has to pay competitors to delay their entry, in most cases it is economically profitable to do so. The settlements arise because generic companies challenge patent of originator producers. Lawsuits can take up to several years and can be expensive for both parties. Hence, settlements often tend to be cheaper and more profitable for both manufacturers (European Commission 2015: 2).

Bohari, Mariuzzo, and Polanski (2015: 4) analyze these pay for delay deals in the context of profitability. They examine that the decision about reverse payment depends on the weakness of the patent, the number of challenges, and most importantly the advantage of competitors for being the first to enter the market. If there are too many possible entrants, originators will not pay to delay entry as costs would be too high (Bohari, Mariuzzo, and Polanski 2015: 5). In their paper, Bohari, Mariuzzo, and Polanski, (2015: 13) regard the reverse payment as a dynamic two stage game. In the first stage one or more generic producers (G_i) can file challenges and the originator manufacturer (B) can offer reverse payment settlements. If G_1 accepts, and G_2 does not accept and wins the litigation, G_2 can enter early in stage one. Then, G_1 can only enter in stage two as G_1 agreed on not entering early. However, B can launch an authorized generic in stage one through G_1, allowing G_1 to enter the market early (first-mover advantage). B, hence, generates additional profits through licensing fees compared to the perfect competitive situation without the launch of a branded generic. In stage two, patents have expired and perfect competition arises as now every generic company is allowed to enter the market (Bohari, Mariuzzo, and Polanski 2015: 10). Following this analysis, originators always offer pay for delay if their profits π_M less cost of delay payment (Y_i) to challengers i exceed the expected profits from either winning challenge litigations with probability ρ or not winning with probability (1-ρ), less the court fees (c_i) for i challenges. In case of winning, the producer generates monopoly profits π_M. In case of losing the manufacturer only generates competition profits π_C.

$$\pi_M - Y_i \geq \rho(\pi_M) + (1-\rho)(\pi_C) - c_i \qquad (4.1)$$

A generic challenger on the other hand will accept the settlement offer if the revenue from pay for delay settlement π_{GiS} plus the payment to settle Y_i exceed the generic producer's expected profits from either not winning the challenge litigations with probability ρ or winning with probability *(1-ρ)*, less the cost for challenging. In case of winning, the generic producers generate market exclusivity profits of π_{GiM}. In case of losing the generic manufacturers only generate competition profits π_{GiC} (Bohari, Mariuzzo, and Polanski 2015: 15).

$$\pi_{GiS} + Y_i \geq \rho(\pi_{GiC}) + (1-\rho)(\pi_{GiM}) - c_i \qquad (4.2)$$

Hence, Bohari, Mariuzzo, and Polanski (2015: 30) state that a pay for delay deal is always profitable if the payment is significantly large enough concerning weak patents. Payments through not launching authorized generics can be profitable in case of high first mover advantages, as generics fear competition during their exclusivity period.

The problem in this case is that there are different jurisdictions of courts, whether pay for delay should be handled to be per se illegal or analyzed according to rule of reason approaches. Until the year 2013, reverse payment settlements were approved by US Court to be part of a patent's scope. It was a manufacturer's right to file infringement litigations, patent protection and find extrajudicial agreements (Peritz 2013: 166). In 2013, the question of violating antitrust law, however, was analyzed more closely by regulators. The first analysis was based on a pay for delay settlement between Actavis and Solvay Pharma. Actavis applied for market approval of its generic substitute to the patented testosterone drug Androgel, produced by Solvay Pharma. Consequently, Solvay Pharma sued Actavis for infringement of patent rights as Androgel was still patent protected. Instead of waiting for litigation to be solved by court, Solvay Pharma offered a settlement transaction of $ 200 million to Actavis to delay entry (Peritz 2013:166). Subsequently, the FTC filed suits against Actavis, claiming that the payment in exchange for delay of entry would violate Section 5 of the FTC Act (15 U.S.C. §45), due to restricting competition and denying consumer's access to substitute products (Silber, Lutinski, and Maddock 2014: 2). After the circuit court rejected this claim, referring to payments for settlements to not be part of antitrust scrutiny but to only be a concern of patent rights, the Supreme Court ruled that there exists no per se legality for pay for delay settlements but a rule of reason approach must be undertaken. Moreover, the Supreme Court ruled that anticompetitive outcomes of such settlements should be weighted not only against patent law but also against competition law since consumers have to pay monopoly prices for an extended time and are restricted from accessing cheaper alternatives (Peritz 2013: 166; Carrier, 2014: 7). This is consistent with the findings of Kimbrough and Sheremeta (2013: 285) who claim that pay for delay settlements delay generic entry by 17 months, causing consumers cost of $ 3.5 billion on average. Especially in combination with product hopping, pay for delay settlements can be profitable for producers when market approval has not been granted yet. An example for this is Cephalon's sleeping disorder drug Provigil (modafinil). Cephalon changed Provigil's formulation and named the drug "Nuvigil". Cephalon, however, did not get market approval for Nuvigil before Provigil's patent expired. Hence, Cephalon paid about $ 300 million to the first four generic companies that tried to enter the market to delay entry for six years. Consequently, Cephalon was sued to pay $ 1.2 billion in reparations to consumers who were harmed as their access to substitutes was restricted (FTC 2015).

Contrary to the case of Actavis and Cephalon, cases of pay for delay settlements without monetary transaction were not prosecuted until recently. One reason for this is, according to Carrier (2014: 8), that prohibiting non-monetary payments would reduce the ability of companies to settle in a litigation case. An example for this case is the pay for delay settlement between GSK and Teva. Facing generic entry by Teva's substitute to GSK's antiepileptic drug Lamictal (lamotrigin), GSK offered Teva to not launch an authorized generic in exchange for Teva delaying market entry (Silverman 2015). In case of pay for delay settlements through agreement on not launching authorized generic, some courts found that antitrust scrutiny would not be applicable as no monetary transaction was made and the delay only affected a short amount of time. In addition to that, jurisdiction decided that plaintiffs had to prove antitrust violation and monopoly power by presenting the value a pay for delay settlement had for defendants. The justification of courts behind this was, that the delay of generic entry was not made in order to induce monopoly prices but helped companies to settle extrajudicially (Carrier 2014: 8-9). In June 2015, however, the US Supreme Court decided that pay for delay settlements involving non-monetary transactions, such as not launching branded generics, have to be analyzed more closely according to rule of reason approaches (Silverman, 2015). Thus, the FTC started suing companies that performed payments involving authorized generics as they harm consumers by delaying generic entry and denying access to cheaper alternative drugs (Walker and Hufford 2016).

In Europe, on the other hand, pay for delay settlements are ruled more strictly. Since 2009 they are regarded as defying competition law per se. An example for this is the Johnson&Johnson and Novartis case in which both generic producers agreed to delay the launch of their fentanyl drug and were fined about € 16 million for violating Article 101 TFEU (European Commission 2013). According to the European Commission (2015: 9) the effect of punishing pay for delay settlements was significant since settlements with payment for delay decreased from 22% of all settlements in 2008 to 12% of all settlements in 2014. It must be noted, however, that settlements restricting competition, but not including monetary transactions (e.g. authorized generics) have risen from 26% in 2008 to 39% in 2014 (European Commission 2015: 9). This might be the case as particularly reverse settlements including monetary transactions are targeted by the European Commission.

Even if the US and EU courts pursued and prosecuted antitrust scrutiny of reverse payment settlements more strictly in the last decade, leading to a reduction in pay for delay settlements, there are still many loopholes in law. Due to antitrust complexity, brand manufacturers can still influence time of generic entry and circumvent statutory provisions. This circumvention, therefore, has to be analyzed more closely in prospective researches concerning benefits for consumers. Peritz (2013: 170) states in this context, that consumers can benefit in the long run, as branded drug producers have higher incentives to innovate when being able to achieve extended market exclusivity. As a result, consumers would benefit from a wider product portfolio when pay for delay is not persecuted. Nonetheless, Peritz (2013: 170) also remarks, that pay for delay leads to less launches of generic substitutes. He claims that competition itself could create incentives to innovate without consumers bearing increased cost of extended patent protection. Therefore, a rule of reason approach must weigh the benefits for consumers against the increases cost for consumers as result of delayed competition entry.

4.2 Merger and Acquisition

In many cases, actions that inhibit competition infringe EU and US antitrust law and are therefore difficult to implement. In several of the before analyzed cases, market complexity helps originator manufacturers to obscure antitrust violations and to circumvent regulatory provision in order to achieve extended market exclusivity. In some cases, participating companies are not pursued for these actions as they do not directly violate competition law. Hence, these actions do not find significant public attention. The following action, however, belongs to the most popular ways to influence competition and is often used, not only by pharmaceutical companies but also by companies active in other markets (Tripathy and Prajapati 2015: 2; Banerjee and Nayak 2015: 490). This action concerns consolidations between two or more companies to gain higher market shares than competitors. The consolidations can affect vertically competing, horizontally competing or else non-competing companies with conglomerate relationships (Tripathy and Prajapati 2015: 5). As vertical restraints, including vertical consolidations, have already been discussed in chapter 3, and conglomerate consolidations do not directly affect competition issues that are analyzed in this paper, I focus on examining horizontal consolidations under the term Merger and Acquisition (M&A) only. In the case of M&A two companies either merge to create a new entity - the "merger" part of M&A – or, in the case of acquisitions, one company purchases a significant number of shares (about 50% or more) of the other one to be majority shareholder. Through M&A, at least one of the consolidating firms who were formerly completely self-governing give up parts of their autonomy to be integrated (Piesse et al. 2013: 441). M&A processes can involve brand name and generic producers, only brand name producers or only generic producers. Nevertheless, I solely focus on M&As between originator manufacturers and generic manufacturers as this is a way to thwart competition.

After patent expiration generic entry reduces market shares of the incumbent, leading to reduction in profits. At a certain point in a branded drug's life-time, generic competition might not be evitable. Hence, brand manufacturers pursue the goal of keeping high market shares when competition begins. M&As with generic competitors can help the brand producer to extend market shares and reduce shares of other generic competitors (Varol, Costa-Font, and McGuire 2011: 7). Moreover, merging with the first market entrant can deter competition and allow originator companies to keep monopoly power (Garnier and Trinquard 2010: 297). Since generic manufacturers face less cost of innovation and realize high cash-flows if they have first-mover advantages, originator manufacturers can use those cash-flows to reinvest in R&D and establish a second mainstay. Generic producers, on the other hand, favor M&As with branded drug producers since profits during patent protection are relatively high compared to generic profits. Besides, brand loyal consumers are more willing to purchase a generic substitute from a brand producing company leading to increased revenues of the merged company (Karval 2006: 279). Cefis and Marsili (2015: 699) state additionally, that M&As can lead to cost reductions through sharing resources and allows the merging parties to access further resources. In the case of Teva, a generic producer, acquiring the originator manufacturer Ivax Corp. in 2005, for example, it was the generic company's interest to generate monopoly profits in addition to its generic profits and access brand loyal customers (Karval 2006: 279). Following this, it can also be profitable for the generic producer to merge.

Moreover, Garnier and Trinquard (2010: 298) conclude that the launch of authorized generics is important for M&As as they decrease the profit of the first entrant, making the generic producer more willing to accept M&A offers. In this case, M&A can be used as a sort of payment to delay entry, similar to pay for delay settlements. Based on the analysis of Garnier (2008: 1866-1869) who examines the incentives for and cost of mergers, Garnier and Trinquard (2010: 298) analyze economic incentives for branded drug companies to deter entry by merging, and the incentive for generic companies to accept those merging offers. Garnier and Trinquard (2010: 298) take the position that only one generic company can enter at a time which is consistent with the exclusivity time for the first generic entrant. Underlying the assumption of M&A to be a Stackelberg model with price competition they find out that M&A depends on the discount rates of the payment and sunk costs the entrant has to spend to enter the market (Garnier and Trinquard, 2010: 298). According to their model, branded firms can decide to either perform M&A with the generic entrant, deter entry through predatory pricing or allow entry. Garnier and Trinquard (2010: 299) test the economic outcomes with and without the launch of a pseudo generic and state that launching a pseudo generic is always more profitable for the originator company which I showed in more detail in chapter 3.3.1. One of the main assumptions of their model is that generic substitutes offer a smaller utility for consumers as they impose switching costs to brand loyal consumers. Hence, consumers get a discounted utility from generic use leaving their utility function being dependent on the price they pay for the respective drug and their utility. The utility is discounted by factor φ, as this factor describes the type of customer on an interval [0,1]. (Garnier and Trinquard 2010: 299):

$$U_B = u - p_B \tag{4.3}$$

$$U_G = \varphi u - p_G \tag{4.4}$$

Assuming that the brand manufacturer launches an authorized generic, the originator firm captures half of the generic's market share. This leads to a profit of the market share of the branded drug x_B times the price the originator producer receives p_B, plus half of the generic market share x_G times the generic price p_G because of Bertrand competition.

$$\pi_B^{Comp} = x_B p_B + \frac{1}{2} x_G p_G \tag{4.5}$$

The generic profit in this case is half of the generic market share times the price for the generic drug, less the cost of entry.

$$\pi_G^{Comp} = \frac{1}{2} x_G p_G - F \tag{4.6}$$

Since Garnier and Trinquard (2010: 301) assume the originator to be a Stackelberg leader, through backward induction, they obtain profits of[26]

$$\pi_B^{Comp} = \frac{5}{8} u \tag{4.7}$$

$$\pi_G^{Comp} = \frac{1}{8} u - F \tag{4.8}$$

In case both companies merge, however, no generic drug enters the market and there is no need to launch an authorized generic. Hence, the merged firm obtains monopoly

26 Note: As this profit is dependent on the indifferent customer φ is omitted in the final profit functions.

power with a market share of x_B=1. Since consumer's utility has to be equal or greater than 0 in order for them to purchase the product, the manufacturer generates a profit of

$$\pi_B{}^M = u \quad (4.9)$$

Knowing that the generic company's profit from not accepting the M&A offer is the generic companies' reservation price, the originator producer offers a merger price that covers the expected profits of the generic manufacturer, including fixed cost to enter the market, discounted to present value.

$$p^{Merger} = \frac{\pi_G^{Comp} + F}{(1-\lambda)} \quad (4.10)$$

The originator's gain from merger is then

$$G_B^M = \frac{\pi_B^M - p^{Merger}}{(1-\lambda)} \quad (4.11)$$

Garnier and Trinquard (2010: 303) conclude, therefore, that the higher the discount factor of future values λ and the higher F, the less profitable M&A is. However, if the discount rate is sufficiently low and entry is sufficiently cheap, it pays off for originator manufacturers to perform M&A. The approach of Garnier and Trinquard gives an idea about a firm's decision to invest in M&A to deter entry. There are, nonetheless, some limits to their findings. Scott-Morton (2002: 139) for example states, that the purchasing price is not the only cost, a company has to bear when performing M&A as both companies have to adjust their organizational framework.

Consistent with the findings of Garnier and Trinquard (2010) that M&A can be profitable for originator and generic producers, Scott-Morton (2002: 143) proves that there exists a significant amount of companies producing brand name and generic drugs. In addition to that, many consolidations between brand manufacturers and generic producers can be observed. One of the biggest and most recent announcement of M&A between brand and generic producers is the case of Pfizer Inc. and Allergan Inc.. In November 2015 the US pharmaceutical originator company Pfizer Inc. announced a consolidation with the Irish generic and branded drug manufacturer Allergan, involving a merger worth more than $ 160 billion (Coons and Cortez 2015). However, this merger announcement does not involve two directly competing companies as the products they offer are no direct competing substitutes and the motivation was not to deter entry but save costs. With this merger, Pfizer would be able to relocate its headquarters to Ireland in order to have its headquarters in a tax cheaper country. The idea behind it is, according to Pfizer, that through savings in taxes Pfizer generates higher profits which they will use to invest in innovation processes (Crow, Fontanella-Khan, and Jopson 2015). In April 2016, however, Pfizer and Allergan decided to not merge because new US tax regulations deterred Pfizer from realizing tax reductions when merging (Thomas and Bray 2016). Even though no merger was performed, this case gives an indication why it can be profitable for manufacturers to perform M&A and how consumers can benefit from such mergers. Similar cases in which the merger was successful are the cases of Teva merging with Ivax and Actavis acquiring Allergan. Both M&As were performed to generate a company with a mixed and wider breadth of product portfolio and not directly to deter entry of competitors (Teva Pharmaceuticals Industries Ltd. 2006; Allergan Inc. 2015).

Even as Garnier and Trinquard (2010: 303) were able to show that M&A can be profitable to deter entry, in my research, I could not find a case where M&A was performed to directly deter entry. In this context, Scott-Morton (2002: 136) who analyzed horizontal M&As between generic and brand manufacturers was also not able to prove entry deterring effects subject to M&As. I affiliate this back to the legal aspects of horizontal M&As. Both, the US antitrust law and the European competition law restrict consolidations that lead to increased market power, reducing competition (Article 101 TFEU; 102 TFEU; 15 U.S.C §1-§2). As M&As between an originator and generic company offering homogenous products would likely be forbidden by the FTC and the European Commission because of violating competition and antitrust law, generic and brand manufacturers are inhibited to perform such mergers.

Nonetheless, M&As can be used to indirectly deter entry. If a pharmaceutical company possesses a generic and a brand division, the company can easily produce authorized generics. The generic division can therefore be used to produce authorized generics and launch them in order to restrict generic competition and retain high market shares (Berndt, et al. 2007: 790). In this case entry is restricted without violation of antitrust law as described in chapter 3.3.1. Furthermore, the consolidation does not only serve deterrence of competition but can also increase innovation and companies' possibilities to access scarce resources. This, consequently, reduce production cost (Cefis and Marsili 2015: 699). However, the innovation effects of M&As are often discussed in literature and no final statement about welfare effects can be made as researchers found both, positive effects of R&D, as well as negative effects on R&D and welfare (Morgan 2001: 182).

Since the outcomes of M&As cannot be standardized, regulators should weigh positive R&D effects, which in long-run serve consumers due to new and enhanced treatments, to the negative effects of creating larger companies with market dominant positions.

5. Conclusion

This publication studies whether actions in restraint of competition always harm consumers and if not, under what circumstances positive welfare effects for consumers emerge. Antitrust laws and regulatory provisions, which can vary significantly across countries, and the complexity of the pharmaceutical market structure influence the market exclusivity time of originator manufacturers. As innovators spend about a billion of revenues on average on the development of new compounds, patent protection grants them a 20-year period of market exclusivity to generate profits for covering innovation costs.
Especially during the past few decades, generic drug producers have found ways to circumvent the patents in order to enter the market early, adding to the availability of parallel traded drugs while branded drugs are still patent protected. Hence, it is in the originators interest to thwart this generic and parallel trade competition. Regulators on the other hand favor the early competition for branded drug producers, as healthcare costs can be reduced because alternative drugs are available for cheaper prices.
There exists a multitude of anticompetitive actions performed by manufacturers to deter generic and parallel traded drugs' market entry. These actions, however, affect welfare in different ways and to different extents. In this publication, I showed that vertical restraints are the most welfare harming actions to deter competition. In particular price discrimination and RPM deter parallel trade and can even lead to higher prices in low price countries. Dual pricing, vertical integration and product change are also used to deter parallel trade. All three vary in their way of implementation but harm consumers to that extend, that no cheaper alternative drugs are available and parallel trade is not feasible anymore. Hence, these actions are forbidden by law and persecuted strictly.
However, I also showed that there exist ways for manufacturers to deter competition of cheaper substitutes that are feasible by circumventing regulatory provisions but also have negative welfare effects. Not launching drugs in low price countries is the respective action. Parallel trade and price reduction due to reference pricing is omitted when no cheaper originator substitute is available in low price countries. In this case two consumer groups are harmed as high price country consumers have to pay high prices and low price country consumers are not able to access the product at all.
In contrast to these actions where there are only negative welfare effects, I showed that there exist actions in which consumers can also benefit from the anti-competitiveness of originator producers. The launch of pseudo-generics for example grants consumers access to a cheaper version of the originator drug in most times even before market

exclusivity time terminated. In case of product hopping consumers can benefit if both versions of the drug remain available on the market and they are not coerced to purchase the more expansive drug version. Strategic patenting, moreover, can be specifically beneficial for consumers with rare diseases where innovation would not take place otherwise as costs would be too high.

In addition, the overview I presented in chapter 2.5 outlines all these possibilities to deter competition and shows that they can even interact with each other. Furthermore, I found out that the competition infringing actions often emerge from one another. Product hopping and the launch of pseudo-generic drugs is not persecuted by regulating authorities, most of the time. This is an indication to further study whether the benefit for consumers outweighs the competition deterring effects with these actions, in order to find possible regulation targets to reduce healthcare expenditures. A more specific example for the difference in strictness of persecution is the pay for delay case. Pay for delay settlements that involve non-monetary transactions have been persecuted less strictly than the ones that involve monetary transactions. As negative effects on consumers, however, are the same in both ways, namely that they are not able to access cheaper alternative drugs, future research should lay a more specific focus on pay for delay settlements that include an agreement to not launch pseudo-generics and study in which cases these settlements should be persecuted more strictly.

In conclusion it is important to note that even though anticompetitive actions have negative welfare effects in most times, I was able to prove that there exist actions which can be beneficial for consumers. As long run and short run impacts on welfare can differ, however, future research should examine further in which cases positive welfare effects outweigh the anticompetitive effects that occur when originator producers infringe competition and are therefore beneficial for consumers.

Bibliography

Abbott, T. A. and J. A. Vernon (2007), 'The Cost of US Pharmaceutical Price Regulation: A Financial Simulation Model of R&D Decisions', *Managerial and Decision Economics* 28, 293-306.

ACEA - European Automobile Manufacturers Association (2015), *The Automobile Industry Pocket Guide 2015-2016,* ACEA, Brussels.

Acemoglu, D., S. Johnson, and T. Mitton (2009), 'Determinants of Vertical Integration: Financial Development and Contracting Costs', *The Journal of Finance* 64, 1251-1290.

Adams, C. P. and V.V. Brantner (2006), 'Estimating The Cost of New Drug Development: Is It Really $802 Million?', *Health Affairs* 25 (2), 420-428.

Adriaen, M., K. De Witte, and S. Simoens (2008), 'Pricing Strategies of Originator and Generic Medicines Following Patent Expiry in Belgium', *Journal of Generic Medicines* 5, 175-187.

Arcidiacono, P., P. B. Ellickson, P. Landry, and D.B. Ridley (2013), 'Pharmaceutical Followers', *International Journal of Industrial Organization* 31, 538-553.

Banerjee, T. and A. Nayak (2015), 'Comparing Domestic and Cross-Border Mergers and Acquisitions in the Pharmaceutical Industry', *Atlantic Economic Journal* 43, 489-499.

Bang, S. H. and Y. Jin (2015), 'Brand-Specificity of Pre-Sale Services and Inter-Brand Competition with Resale Price Maintenance', *International Review of Law and Economics* 43, 1-9.

Bansal, I. S., S. Deeptymaja, G. Bakshi, and S. Singh (2009), 'Evergreening- A Controversial Issue in the Pharma Milieu', *Journal of Intellectual Property Rights* 14, 299-306.

Bardey, D., A. Bommier, and B. Jullien (2010), 'Retail Price Regulation and Innovation: Reference Pricing in the Pharmaceutical Industry', *Journal of Health Economics* 29, 303-316.

Bart, T. N. (2008), 'Parallel Trade of Pharmaceuticals: A Review of Legal, Economic, and Political Aspects' *Value in Health* 11, 996-1005.

Bechah, Y., C. Capo, J.-L. Mege, and D. Raoult (2008), 'Epidemic Typhus', *The Lancet Infectious Diseases* 8, 417-426.

Bennato, A. R., and T. Valletti (2014), 'Pharmaceutical Innovation and Parallel Trade', *International Journal of Industrial Organization* 33, 83-92.

Berndt, E. R., R. Mortimer, A. Bhattacharjya, A. Parece, and E. Tuttle (2007), 'Authorized Generic Drugs, Price Competition, And Consumers' Welfare', *Health Affairs* 26, 790-799.

Birg, L. (2015), 'Externalities of National Pharmaceutical Policy When Markets are Integrated Through Parallel Trade', *Review of International Economics* 23, 558-574.

Blind, K., K. Cremers, and E. Mueller, (2009), 'The Influence of Strategic Patenting on Companies' Patent Portfolios', *Research Policy* 38, 428-436.

Bohari, F. A., F. Mariuzzo, and A. Polanski (2015), 'Entry Limiting Agreements for Pharmaceuticals: Pay-to-Delay and Authorized Generic Deals', *CCP Working Paper No.15-5,* Center for Competition Policy, Norwich.

Bonett, C. and P. Dubois (2010), 'Inference on Vertical Contracts Between Manufacturers and Retailers Allowing for Nonlinear Pricing and Resale Price Maintenance', *RAND Journal of Economics* 41, 139-164.

Bower, A. B., S. Landreth Grau, and V. A. Taylor (2013), 'Over-the-counter vs. prescription medications: are consumer perceptions of the consequences of drug instruction non-compliance different?', *International Journal of Consumer Studies* 37, 228-233.

Brekke, K. R. and M. Kuhn (2006), 'Direct to Consumer Advertising in Pharmaceutical Markets', *Journal of Health Economics* 25, 102-130.

Brekke, K. R., A. L. Grasdal, and T.H. Holmas (2009), 'Regulation and Pricing of Pharmaceuticals: Reference Pricing or Price Cap Regulation', *European Economic Review* 53, 170-185.

Brekke, K. R., T. H. Holmas, and O.R. Straume (2015), 'Price Regulation and Parallel Imports of Pharmaceuticals', *Journal of Public Economics* 129, 92-105.

Brekke, K. R., T.H. Holmas, and O.R. Straume (2011), 'Reference Pricing, Competition and Pharmaceutical Expenditures: Theory and Evidence from a natural Experiment', *Journal of Public Economics* 95, 624-638.

Carrier, M. A. (2010), 'A Real-World Analysis of Pharmaceutical Settlements: The Missing Dimension of Product Hopping', *Florida Law Review* 62, 1009-1036.

Carrier, M. A. (2014), 'Pharmaceutical Antitrust Complexity', *CPI Antitrust Chronicle 2*, Competition Policy International, Boston.

Cefis, E. and O. Marsili (2015), 'Crossing the Innovation Threshold Through Mergers and Acquisitions', *Research Policy* 44, 698- 710.

Chae, S. and P. Heidhues (2004), 'Buyers' Alliances for Bargaining Power', *Journal of Economics and Management Strategy* 13, 731-754.

Chakrabarti, R., C. Ramos, and S. Henneberg (2013), 'Network Dynamics in the UK Pharmaceutical Network - A Network-As-Practice Perspective', *Industrial Marketing Management* 42, 356-371.

Chen, J. (2008), 'An Antitrust Analysis of Product Hopping in the Pharmaceutical Industry', *Columbia Law Review* 104, 1471-1515.

Chen, Y. and K. E. Maskus (2005), 'Vertical Pricing and Parallel Imports', *Journal of International Trade and Economic Development* 14, 1-18.

Chin, A. T. (2010), 'Consumer Learning and Heterogeneity: Dynamics of Demand for Prescription Drugs After Patent Expiration', *International Journal of Industrial Organization* 28, 619-638.

Cockburn, I. M. and R. M. Henderson (2001), 'Publicly Founded Science and the Productivity of the Pharmaceutical Industry', in: A. B. Jaffe, J. Lerner, and S. Stern (eds.), *Innovation Policy and the Economy,* Vol. 1, MIT Press, Cambridge, MA, pp. 1-34.

Comanor, W. S. and F. M. Scherer (2013), 'Mergers and Innovation in the Pharmaceutical Industry', *Journal of Health Economics* 32, 106–113.

Costa-Font, J., A. McGuire, and N. Varol (2014), 'Price Regulation and Relative Delays in Generic Drug Adoption', *Journal of Health Economics* 38, 1-9.

Costa-Font, J., C. Rudisill, and S. Tan (2014), 'Brand Loyalty, Patients and Limited Generic Medicines Uptake', *Health Policy* 116, 224-233.

Csiszár, P. (2012), 'Delay in Generic Entry Should Remain a Concern to Competition Authorities', *Journal of Generic Medicine* 9, 123-127.

Danzon, P. M. and M. F. Furukawa (2008), 'International Prices and Availability of Pharmaceuticals in 2005', *Health Affairs* 27, 221-233.

Danzon, P. M., A. W. Mulcahy, and A. K. Towse (2015), 'Pharmaceutical Pricing in Emerging Markets: Effects of Income, Competition and Procurement', *Health Economics* 24, 235-252.

Danzon, P. M., R. Y. Wang, and L. Wang (2005), 'The Impact of Price Regulation on the Launch Delay of New Drugs: Evidence from Twenty-Five Major Markets in the 1990s', *Health Economics* 14, 269-296.

De Frutosa, M.-A., C. Ornaghib, and G. Siotis (2013), 'Competition in the Pharmaceutical Industry: How do Quality Differences Shape Advertising Strategies?', *Journal of Health Economics* 32, 268-285.

DiMasi, J. A. (2002), 'The Value of Improving the Productivity of the Drug Development Process: Faster Times and Better Decisions', *PharmacoEconomics* 20, 1-10.

DiMasi, J. A. and H. G. Grabowski (2007), 'The Cost of Biopharmaceutical R&D: Is Biotech Different?', *Managerial and Decision Economics* 28, 469–479.

DiMasi, J. A., R. W. Hansen, and H. G. Grabowski (2003), 'The Price of Innovation: New Estimates of Drug Development Costs', *Journal of Health Economics* 22, 151-185.

Dubois, P., O. De Mouzon, F. Scott-Morton, and P. Seabright (2015), 'Market Size and Pharmaceutical Innovation', *RAND Journal of Economics* 46, 844-871.

Duso, T., A. Herr, and M. Suppliet (2014), 'The Welfare Impact of Parallel Imports: A Structural Approach Applied to the German Market for Oral Anti-Diabetics', *Health Economics* 23, 1036-1057.

Dwivedi, G., S. Hallihosur, and L. Rangan (2010), 'Evergreening: A Deceptive Device in Patent Rights', *Technology in Society* 32, 324-330.

EFPIA - European Federation of Pharmaceutical Industries and Associations (2015), *The Pharmaceutical Industry in Figures: Key Data 2015,* EFPIA, Brussels.

European Commission (2015), *The 2015 EU R&D Industrial Investment Scoreboard,* European Commission, Brussels.

European Commission (2015), '6th Report on the Monitoring of Patent Settlements', *European Commission Report* 6, Brussels.

Fisher Ellison, S. and C. M. Snyder (2010), 'Countervailing Power in Wholesale Pharmaceuticals', *Journal of Industrial Economics* 58, 32-53.

Foros, Ø., H. J. Kind, and G. Shaffer (2011), 'Resale Price Maintenance and Restrictions on Dominant Firm and Industry-Wide Adoption', *International Journal of Industrial Organization* 29, 179-186.

Galizzi, M. M., S. Ghislandi, and M. Miraldo (2011), 'Effects of Reference Pricing in Pharmaceutical Markets', *PharmacoEconomics* 29, 17-33.

Garattini, L., N. Motterlini, and D. Cornago (2008), 'Prices and Distribution Margins of In-Patent Drugs in Pharmacy: A Comparison in Seven European Countries', *Health Policy* 85, 305-313.

Garnier, L. (2008), 'Endogenous Mergers and Cost Heterogeneity', *Applied Economics* 40, 1865–1871.

Garnier, L. and S. Trinquard (2010), 'Entry Deterrence and Mergers under Price Competition in Pharmaceutical Markets', *Applied Economics* 42, 297–309.

Ghislandi, S. (2011), 'Competition and the Reference Pricing Scheme for Pharmaceuticals', *Journal of Health Economics* 30, 1137-1149.

Gilbert, R. (2007), 'Holding Innovation to an Antitrust Level', *Competition Policy International Journal* 3, 47-77.

Gilbert, R. J. (2015), 'Not Another Drug! Antitrust for Drug and other Innovations' *Antitrust* 30, 38-45.

Ginsburg, D. H., K. W. Wong-Ervin, and J. D. Wright (2015), 'Product Hopping and the Limits of Antitrust: The Danger of Micromanaging Innovation', *CPI Antitrust Chronicle* 1, Competition Policy International, Boston.

Giovannetti, E. and L. Magazzini (2013), 'Resale Price Maintenance: An Empirical Analysis of UK Firms' Compliance', *The Economic Journal* 123, F582-F535.

Goldman, D. P., D. N. Lakdawalla, J. D. Malkin, J. Romley, and T. Philipson (2011), 'The Benefits From Giving Makers Of Conventional 'Small Molecule' Drugs Longer Exclusivity Over Clinical Trial Data', *Health Affairs* 30, 84-90.

Gonzalez, J., C. Sismeiro, S. Dutta, and P. Stern (2008), 'Can Branded Drugs Benefit from Generic Entry? The Role of Detailing and Price in Switching to Non-Bioequivalent Molecules', *International Journal of Research in Marketing* 25, 247-260.

Grabowski, H. G. and M. Kyle (2007), 'Generic Competition and Market Exclusivity Periods in Pharmaceuticals', *Managerial and Decision Economics* 28, 491-502.

Grabowski, H. G. and J. Moe (2008), 'Impact of Economic, Regulatory, and Patent Policies on Innovation in Cancer Chemoprevention', *Cancer Prevention Research* 1, 84-90.

Grabowski, H. G. and R. Y. Wann (2008), 'Do Faster Food and Drug Administration Drug Reviews Adversely Affect Patient Safety? An Analysis of the 1992 Prescription Drug User Fee Act', *Journal of Law and Economics* 51, 377-406.

Graslandt, M. and K. E. Maskus (2004), 'Parallel Imports and the Pricing of Pharmaceutical Products: Evidence from the European Union', *Journal of Health Economics* 23, 1035-1057.

Graslandt, M. and K. E. Maskus (2007), 'Vertical Distribution, Parallel Trade, and Price Divergence in Integrated Markets', *European Economic Review* 51, 943-970.

Grossman, G. M. and E. L.-C. Lai (2008), 'Parallel Imports and Price Controls', *The RAND Journal of Economics* 39, 378-402.

Guido, G., G. Pino, S. Superiore, D. Frangipane (2011), 'The Role of Credibility and Perceived Image of Supermarket Stores as Valuable Providers of Over-The-Counter Drugs', *Journal of Marketing Management* 27, 207-224.

Guo, S., B. Hu, and H. Zhong (2013), 'Impact of Parallel Trade on Pharmaceutical Firms' Profits: Rise or Fall?', *European Journal of Health Economics* 14, 345-355.

Gupta, H., S. Kumar, S. K. Roy, and R. S. Gaud (2010), 'Patent Protection Strategies' *Journal of Pharmacy and BioAllied Science* 2, 2-7.

Harrhoff, D. and M. Reitzig (2004), 'Determinants of Opposition Against EPO Patent Grants - the Case of Biotechnology and Pharmaceuticals', *International Journal of Industrial Organization* 20, 443-480.

Hemphill, C. S. and B. N. Sampat (2012), 'Evergreening, Patent Challenges, and Effective Market Life in Pharmaceuticals', *Journal of Health Economics* 31, 327-339.

Hollis, A. (2005), 'How do Brands' "Own Generics" Affect Pharmaceutical Prices?', *Review of Industrial Organization* 27, 329–350.

Hollis, A. (2002), 'The Importance of Being First: Evidence from Canadian Generic Pharmaceuticals', *Health Economics* 11, 723-734.

Hosken, D. and B. Wendling (2013), 'Informing the Uninformed: How Drug Advertising Affects Check-Up Visits', *International Journal of Industrial Organization* 31, 181-194.

Hudson, J. (2000), 'Generic Take-Up in the Pharmaceutical Market Following Patent Expiry: A Multi-Country Study', *International Review of Law and Economics* 20, 205-221.

Hull, D. W. and M. J. Clancy (2016), 'The Application of EU Competition Law in the Pharmaceutical Sector', *Journal of European Competition Law and Practice* 7, 150-161.

Huskamp, H. A., J. M. Donohue, C. Koss, E. R. Berndt, and R. G. Frank (2008), 'Generic Entry, Reformulations and Promotion of SSRIs in the US', *PharmacoEconomics* 26, 603-616.

IFPMA - International Federation of Pharmaceutical Manufacturers & Associations (2014), *The Pharmaceutical Industry and Global Health,* IFPMA, Geneva.

IMS Health - Institute for Healthcare Informatics (2014), *Global Outlook for Medicines Through 2018,* IMS Health, Parsippany, NJ.

Jaffe, S. (2015), 'USA Grapples with High Drug Costs', *The Lancet* 386, 2127-2128.

Jambulingam, T., R. Kathuria, and J. R. Nevin (2009), 'How Fairness Garners Loyalty in the Pharmaceutical Supply Chain Role of Trust in the Wholesaler-Pharmacy Relationship', *International Journal of Pharmaceutical and Healthcare Marketing* 3, 305-322.

Jelovac, I. and C. Bordoy (2005), 'Pricing and Welfare Implications of Parallel Imports in the Pharmaceutical Industry', *International Journal of Healthcare Finance and Economics* 5, 5-21.

Jullien, B. and P. Rey (2007), 'Resale Price Maintenance and Collusion', *RAND Journal of Economics* 38, 983-1001.

Königbauer, I. (2007), 'Advertising and Generic Market Entry', *Journal of Health Economics* 26, 286-305.

Kaiser, U., S. J. Mendez, T. Rønde, and H. Ullrich (2014), 'Regulation of Pharmaceutical Prices: Evidence from a Reference Price Reform in Denmark', *Journal of Health Economics* 36, 174-187.

Kanavos, P. and J. Costa-Font (2005), 'Pharmaceutical Parallel Trade in Europe: Stakeholder and Competition Effects', *Economic Policy* 20, 751-798.

Kanavos, P. and S. Vandoros (2010), 'Competition in Prescription Drug Markets: Is Parallel Trade the Answer?', *Managerial and Decision Economics* 31, 325-338.

Karval, V. (2006), 'The Changing Competitive Landscape in the Global Generics Market: Threat or Opportunity?', *Journal of Generic Medicines* 3, 269–279.

Kesselheim, A. S., L. Murtagh, L. and M. M. Mello (2011), '"Pay for Delay" Settlements of Disputes Over Pharmaceutical Patents', *The New England Journal of Medicine* 365, 1439-1445.

Kimbrough, E. O., and R. M, Sheremeta (2013), 'Side-Payments and the Costs of Conflict', *International Journal of Industrial Organization* 31, 278-286.

Kong, J. and J. R. Seldon (2004), 'Pseudo-Generic Products and Barriers to Entry in Pharmaceutical Markets', *Review of Industrial Organization* 25, 71-86.

Kucuk, S. U. and H. J. Timmermans (2012), 'Resale Price Maintenance (RPM): The U.S. and E.U. Perspectives', *Journal of Retailing and Consumer Services* 19, 537-544.

Kyle, M. K. (2007), 'Pharmaceutical Price Controls and Entry Strategies', *The Review of Economics and Statistics* 89, 88-99.

Kyle, M. K., J. S. Allsbrook and K. A. Schulman (2008), 'Does Reimportation Reduce Price Differences for Prescription Drugs? Lessons from the European Union', *Health Service Research* 43, 1308-1324.

Lafontaine, F. and M. Slade (2007), 'Vertical Integration and Firm Boundaries: The Evidence', *Journal of Economic Literature* 45, 629-685.

Lanjouw, J. O. and M. Schankermann (2001), 'Characteristics of Patent Litigation: A Window on Competition', *RAND Journal of Economics* 32, 129-151.

Leopold, C., S. Vogler, A. Mantel-Teeuwisse, K. De Joncheere, H. Leufkens, and R. Laing. (2012), 'Differences in External Price Referencing in Europe - A Descriptive Overview', *Health Policy* 104, 50-60.

Li, C. and K. E. Maskus (2006), 'The impact of Parallel Imports on Investments in Cost-Reducing Research and Development', *International Economics* 68, 433-455.

Li, C. and J. Robles (2007), 'Product Innovation and Parallel Trade', *International Journal of Industrial Organization* 25, 417-429.

Lichtenberg, F. R. and T. J. Philipson (2002), 'The Dual Effects of Intellectual Property Regulations: Within-and Between-Competition in the US Pharmaceuticals Industry', *NBER Working Paper No. 9303,* NBER, Cambridge, MA.

Mathewson, F. and R. Winter (1998), 'The Law and Economics of Resale Price Maintenance', *Review of Industrial Organization* 13, 57-84.

Matteucci, G. and P. Reverberi (2016), 'Some Unintended Consequences of Parallel Trade in Pharmaceuticals', *Managerial and Decision Economics* 37, 50-61.

Moloshok, M. (2007), 'Dr. Miles - A Rock of Ages', *The Antitrust Source* 2, 13-19.

Moore, S. and R. Montagnon (2010), 'AstraZeneca's SPC and Deregistration Practices 'Abuses of Dominant Position', *Journal of Intellectual Property Law & Practice* 5, 687-689.

Morgan, E. J. (2001), 'Innovation and Merger Decisions in the Pharmaceutical Industry', *Review of Industrial Organization* 19, 181-197.

Ostwald, D. A., K. Zubrzycki, and J. L. Knippel (2015), 'The Economic Footprint of the Pharmaceutical Economy- Research Report 2015', *WifOR Research Report*, WifOR, Darmstadt.

Parker, S. and K. Mooney (2007), 'Is "Evergreening" a Cause for Concern? A Legal Perspective', *Journal of Commercial Biotechnology* 13, 235-243.

Pedroso, M. C. and D. Nakano (2009), 'Knowledge and Information Flows in Supplychains: A Study on Pharmaceutical Companies', *International Journal of Production Economics* 122, 376-384.

Peritz, R. J. (2013), 'Taking Antitrust to Patent School: The Instance of Pay-for-Delay Settlements', *The Antitrust Bulletin* 58, 159-171.

Perry, M. K. (1988), 'Vertical Integration: Determinants and Effects', in: R. Schmalensee and R. D. Willig (eds.), *Handbook of Industrial Organization,* Vol. 1, North-Holland, Oxford and Amsterdam pp. 185-224.

Phrma - Pharmaceutical Research and Manufacturers of America (2015), *2015 Profile-Biopharmaceutical Reseach Industry*, Phrma, Washington, DC.

Piesse, J., C.-F. Lee, L. Lin, and H.-C. Kuo (2013), 'Merger and Acquisition: Definitions, Motives, and Market Responses', in: C.-F. Lee, and A. C. Lee (eds.), *Encyclopedia of Finance,* Vol. 2, Springer Science and Business Media, New York, pp. 411-420.

Puig-Junoy, J. (2010), 'Impact of European Pharmaceutical Price Regulation on Generic Price Competition', *PharmacoEconomics* 28, 649-663.

Raff, H. and N. Schmitt (2007), 'Why Parallel Trade may Raise Producers' Profits', *Journal of International Economics* 71, 434-447.

Reiffen, D. and M.R. Ward (2007), '"Branded Generics" as a Strategy to Limit Cannibalization of Pharmaceutical Markets', *Managerial and Decision Economics* 28, 251-265.

Reitzig, M. (2004), Improving Patent Valuations for Management Purposes - Validating New Indicators by Analyzing Application Rationales', *Research Policy* 33, 939-957.

Rey, P. and T. Vergé (2010), 'Resale Price Maintenance and Interlocking Relationships', *The Journal of Industrial Economics* 58, 928-961.

Richard, O. and L. Van Horn (2004), 'Persistence in prescriptions of branded drugs', *International Journal of Industrial Organization* 22, 523-540.

Ruggeri, K. and E. Nolte (2013), *Pharmaceutical Pricing: The Use of External Reference Pricing,* RAND Europe, Pittsburgh.

Schildkraut, M. G. (2004), 'Patent Splitting Settlements and the Reverse Payment Fallacy', *Antitrust Law Journal* 71, 1033-1068.

Schwabe, U. (2015), 'Arzneiverordnungen im Überblick', in: U. Schwabe and D. Paffrath (eds.), *Arzneiverordnungsreport 2015,* Springer-Verlag, Berlin, pp. 3-35.

Scott Morton, F. and K. Margaret (2012), 'Markets for Pharmaceutical Products', in M. V. Pauly, T. G. McGuire, and P. B. Barros (eds.), *Handbook of Health Economics*, Vol. 2, North Holland, Oxford and Amsterdam, pp. 763-823.

Scott-Morton, F. M. (2000), 'Barriers to Entry, Brand Advertising, and Generic Entry in the US Pharmaceutical Industry', *International Journal of Industrial Organization* 18, 1085-1104.

Scott-Morton, F. M. (2002), 'Horizontal Integration Between Brand and Generic Firms in the Pharmaceutical Industry', *Journal of Economics & Management Strategy* 11, 135–168.

Silber, S. and K. Kuritz (2010), 'Product Switching in the Pharmaceutical Industry: Ripe for Antitrust Scrutiny?', *Journal of Generic Medicines* 7, 119-130.

Silber, S., J. Lutinski, and R. Maddock (2014), '"Good Luck" Post-Actavis: Current State of Play on "Pay-for-Delay" Settlements', *CPI Antitrust Chronicle* 2, Competition Policy International, Boston.

Simonet, D. (2007 a), 'Evaluation of Downstream Integration in the US Pharmaceutical Industry', *International Journal of Healthcare and Marketing* 1, 143-158.

Simonet, D. (2007), 'The Strategies of Vertical Integration in the American Pharmaceutical Industry and the Quest for Market Power', *Competition & Change* 11, 19-38.

Sportiello, L., C. Rafaniello, C. Scavone, C. Vitale, F. Rossi, and A. Capuano (2016), 'The Importance of Pharmacovigilance for the Drug Safety: Focus on Cardiovascular Profile of Incretin-Based Therapy', *International Journal of Cardiology* 202, 731-735.

Stargardt, T. (2011), 'Modelling Pharmaceutical Price Changes in Germany: A Function of Competition and Regulation', *Applied Economics* 48, 4515-4526.

Stothers, C. (2010), 'CJ Rules on GSK's 'Dual Pricing' of Pharmaceuticals in Spain', *Journal of European Competition Law and Practices* 1, 123-124.

Stotland Weiswasser, E. and S. D. Danzis (2004), 'The Hatch-Waxman Act: History, Structure, and Legacy', *Antitrust Law Journal* 71, 585-608.

Sultana, J., P. Cutroneo, and G. Trifirò (2013), 'Clinical and Economic Burden of Adverse Drug Reactions', *Journal of Pharmacology and Pharmacotherapeutics* 4, 73-77.

Swinney, D. C. and J. Anthony (2011), 'How were Medicines Discovered?' *Nature Reviews Drug Discovery* 10, 507-519.

Tripathy, S. and V. Prajapati (2015), 'Mergers and Acquisitions: Trends in Indian Pharmaceutical Industry', *Journal of Medical Marketing* 0, 1-9.

Valletti, T. M. (2006), 'Differential Pricing, Parallel Trade, and the Incentive to Invest', *Journal of International Economics* 70, 314-324.

Vandoros, S. and P. Kanavos (2014), 'Parallel Trade and Pharmaceutical Prices: A Game-theoretic Approach and Empirical Evidence from the European Union', *The World Economy* 37, 856-880.

Varol, N., J. Costa-Font, A. McGuire (2011), 'Does Pharmaceutical Price Regulation Affect the Adoption of Generic Competition? Evidence from the OECD, 1999-2008', *CESifo Working Papers No. 3441*, CESifo, London.

Vernon, J. A. (2005), 'Examining the Link Between Price Regulation and Pharmaceutical R&D Investment', *Health Economics* 14, 1-16.

Wang, H. (2004), 'Resale Price Maintenance in an Oligopoly with Uncertain Demand', *International Journal of Industrial Organization* 22, 389-411.

Wharam, J. F., D. Ross-Degnan, and M. B. Rosenthal (2013), 'The ACA and High-Deductible Insurance - Strategies for Sharpening a Blunt Instrument', *The New England Journal of Medicine* 369, 1481-1484.

Wittkowsky, T. X. (2001), 'Intellectual Property and Other Legal Aspects of Drug Repurposing', *Drug Discovery Today: Therapeutic Strategies* 8, 139-143.

Online References

Abboud, L. (2004), 'Drug Makers Use New Tactic to Ding Generic-Drug Firms', URL: http://www.wsj.com/articles/SB107515784029812090 (retrieved May 02, 2016).

Allergan Inc. (2015), 'Actavis Completes Allergan Acquisition', URL: http://goo.gl/Kz0Kab (retrieved April 08, 2016).

CDER - Center for Drug Evaluation Research (1998), 'The CDER Handbook', URL: http://goo.gl/wS4nT4 (retrieved April 14, 2016).

Coons, S. and M. Cortez (2015), 'Pfizer and Allergan to Combine with Joint Value of $160 Billion', URL: http://goo.gl/UDeMwG (retrieved April 25, 2016).

Crow, D., J. Fontanella-Khan, and B. Jopson (2015), 'Pfizer Seeks Washington Support for $160bn Allergan Deal', URL: https://goo.gl/rpgXmm (retrieved April 30, 2016).

European Commission (2013), 'Antitrust: Commission fines Johnson & Johnson and Novartis € 16 million for delaying market entry of generic pain-killer fentanyl', URL: http://goo.gl/zq0TzX (retrieved April 04, 2016).

FTC Bureau of Competition. (2013), 'Agreements Filed with the Federal Trade Commission under the Medicare Prescription Drug, Improvement, and Modernization Act of 2003: Overview of Agreements Filed in FY 2012', URL: https://goo.gl/pKxlFm (retrieved April 21, 2016).

FTC (2015), 'FTC Settlement of Cephalon Pay for Delay Case Ensures $1.2 Billion in Ill-Gotten Gains Relinquished; Refunds Will Go to Purchasers Affected By Anticompetitive Tactics', URL: https://goo.gl/vS0y7s (retrieved April 04, 2016).

Gilbert, J. and P. Rosenberg (2004), 'There's No Such Thing as a Free Drug' URL: http://goo.gl/sJA5sk (retrieved May 03, 2016).

GlaxoSmithKline (2003), 'GlaxoSmithKline, Par Pharmaceutical, Inc. and Pentech Pharmaceuticals, Inc. Agree to Settle Paxil(R) Patent Litigation', URL: http://goo.gl/82dbW8 (retrieved May 01, 2016).

IMS Health - Institute for Healthcare Informatics (2015), 'IMS Health Market Prognosis', URL: http://goo.gl/PBMtXb, (retrieved May 03, 2016).

Perlman, J. (2015), 'Turing Pharmaceuticals Facing NY Antitrust Inquiry in Wake of 5,000 Percent Price Hike' URL: http://goo.gl/DpdPvm (retrieved May 01, 2016).

Silverman, E. (2015), 'Cash is not Always King in Pharma Pay-to-Delay Deals: Appeals Court', URL: http://goo.gl/BtcHrJ (retrieved April 23, 2016).

Simons, J. (2004), 'Lilly Goes Off Prozac: The Drugmaker Bounced Back from the Loss of its Blockbuster, but the Recovery had Costs', URL: http://goo.gl/TWUnSL (retrieved April 29, 2016).

Teva Pharmaceuticals Industries Ltd. (2006), 'Teva Completes Acquisition of Ivax', URL: http://goo.gl/CakRQL (retrieved April 28, 2016).

The Worldbank (2016), 'Population Total', URL: http://goo.gl/HbER3v (retrieved May 02, 2016).

Thomas, K. and C. Bray (2016), 'Pfizer Faces Limited Options After Its Dead Deal with Allergan', URL: http://goo.gl/hUJFvV (retrieved May 30, 2016).

World Health Organization (WHO) (2016), 'Typhus fever (Epidemic louse-borne typhus)', URL: http://goo.gl/hEcUzg (retrieved April 22, 2016).

Walker, J. and A. Hufford (2016), 'FTC Sues Endo, Alleges Company Paid Off Generic Drugmakers', URL: http://goo.gl/cSFNVX (retrieved May 01, 2016)

FSC
www.fsc.org
MIX
Papier | Fördert gute Waldnutzung
FSC® C083411

Kolibri 360 GmbH
Ferdinand-Jühlke-Straße 7
99095 Erfurt, Deutschland
produktsicherheit@kolibri360.de